Magnolia Table

Magnolia Table

A COLLECTION OF RECIPES FOR GATHERING | VOLUME 2

JOANNA GAINES

PHOTOGRAPHY BY AMY NEUNSINGER

WILLIAM MORROW

An Imprint of HarperCollins*Publishers*

also by Joanna Gaines

THE MAGNOLIA STORY

MAGNOLIA TABLE

HOMEBODY

WE ARE THE GARDENERS

HarperCollins books may be purchased for educational,
business, or sales promotional use. For information,
please email the Special Markets Department at
SPsales@harpercollins.com.

FIRST EDITION

Designed by Kelsie Monsen
Photography by Amy Neunsinger
Photograph on pages 4–5 by John and Maura Stoffer
Illustrations by Andre Junget

Library of Congress Cataloging-in-Publication Data
has been applied for.

ISBN 978-0-06-282018-1

20 21 22 23 24   WOR   10 9 8 7 6 5 4 3 2

To my mother:
You have taught me that a
home-cooked meal is a warm
extension of love and care
for your family. Some of my
fondest memories are with
you in the kitchen, and many
of my favorite meals are the
ones you and I have made
side by side.

To my mother-in-law, Gayle:
The way you've always
opened up your home to
family, friends, and even
strangers has inspired
me over the years to be
intentional about the details
when it comes to making
my own dinner table a place
for people to gather and feel
welcome.

Contents

Introduction

It's no secret that I'm a creature of habit. When I find a routine, a rhythm, or really *anything at all* that works and feels right, I cling to it with two steady hands. It is precisely the sure and steady part of my personality that has always been drawn to food, less for the thrill of a really good flavor combination or the plentiful health benefits, both of which I have grown to place great value in, but more because food, to me, has long represented comfort and familiarity. When I've been far from home, or just moved into a *new* home, whipping up a familiar family recipe would instantly give me a sense of place, wherever I happened to be. Ideally in the form of cheesy bread and homemade dumplings—or, better yet, chocolate cake!

Back when Chip and I were young parents, raising four kids under the age of four, food became a survival tool, a physical means of nourishing six bodies three times a day. I longed for *easy,* not new, so I leaned in to the food I grew up with, the no-fail recipes that I could be confident I wouldn't mess up while four hungry babies stared up at me. During those years, dinner was rarely elaborate or impressive. But it was, on most days, the only time we could all sit around the table and be intentional about sharing a meal together. I started to notice a pattern that followed this nightly rhythm: When dinner was served, the house quieted, stories were told, and when it was time to excuse ourselves, everyone was fed in more ways than one. If not for the warm food on the table, those sacred evenings wouldn't have happened. And so, every day, it seemed, I found myself anticipating dinner around the table, which soon turned into thinking ahead about what I might serve and how I could set the table to make dinnertime feel a little more special. And that's when I began to see the kitchen differently—for what it had to offer my family beyond being the place where we stored our produce and stacked our plates. What had once been a place I often dreaded, I now saw as a gift, there to equip me with the space and tools I needed to make these meals possible.

So, slowly, I began to spend more time in our kitchen, messing with ingredients and practicing using new tools and recipes. I was still a ways away from feeling confident in this space, but something deep inside me told me that the life that was happening around our table every night was worth the effort. I started to pay attention to the foods my kids favored and practiced making meals that would support, but also oftentimes challenge, their palates. Gradually, I started to feel like I actually belonged in this space. Though there was, *and still is,* plenty of ordering in on nights when I just don't feel like cooking or when a meal inevitably burns.

That mind-set shift was a pivotal turning point for me. It led me to actually enjoy the creative part of cooking a meal, but even more, it opened my eyes to how much I treasured what came next—when everyone gathered around the table—whether it was among family, friends, or mixed company. Since then, it has been the soul and substance that resounds at the table—of stories being told while glasses clink and hands pass bowls, the excitement that murmurs when I confirm there is in fact dessert tonight, and always the lingering conversations—that has made the table itself one of the most familiar places in my world. The life that unfolds around it day after day continues to be potent enough to draw me back again and again.

My first cookbook, *Magnolia Table,* was a celebration of this very thing, an ode to bringing people around the table with recipes I knew intimately and had used to gather loved ones around my own table for years. From the start, I knew that I wanted to fill its pages with all my favorites: really good, easy-to-execute recipes that I had been relying on for years, including dishes from dear friends or favorite recipes from family traditions. Once that book was put out into the world, and I saw so many of you making the same recipes that have been around my own table, friends' tables, and tables of generations past, it impressed upon me a profound commitment to the value of food being shared, of worn-in recipes being handed down. Watching my family's favorite meals become a part of the fabric of your families taught me so much more than I thought I knew about the power of food. Yes, food is personal. Yes, it can nourish our bodies. But it can also bridge strangers across state lines and beyond language barriers. My family's dinner table became hitched to yours, and yours became hitched to the table of someone entirely new. And the old adage—*a shared table is a shared life*—never felt more true.

But this experience was entirely unlike the first. In short: *This book stretched me.* Because most of my tried-and-true recipes were already out in the world, this process required me to get in the kitchen and start from scratch. This time around, my team and I worked to develop new recipes, which required me to study cooking in a way that I never had in order to learn how to go about refining dishes that I'd always craved but couldn't put a name to. Once again, I was faced with an opportunity to push myself beyond my comfort zone and stretch my palate. On many days, standing in my kitchen flour-clad and deep in recipe development took me back to those early years in my first tiny kitchen, giving myself pep talks when it came to learning how to use new tools and discern ingredients. But just as I eventually realized back then, within the safety of my own walls, I felt free to try and fail and make messes. Both times, confidence was earned by trial and error; and both times have reminded me that a sweet reward of cooking is not only in what's created, but also in the simple act of getting to create. For this, I have become convinced that there should always be space for grace in the kitchen—along with plenty of takeout menus.

While it would certainly be the easy choice to fill a week of dinners with my family's favorite dishes and call it good, deep down that's not what I want for any of us. Taking a chance on ourselves and trying something new is how we get to experience possibility and how we stay enamored with the world around us. Being open to change and growth refines who we are and makes us all more gracious and understanding humans. And who knows, it might even lead to raising kids who become the kind of adults who love to bring people around their own tables.

To me, those things make being stretched worth it, even when it goes against every natural fiber of my being. But because growth by its very nature requires change, and I don't get to have one without the other—they are wisely and intricately woven together—it means being willing to learn from those who know more than I do, and to invite my food tastes and preferences to evolve.

So that's what I did. I tried and failed, and I tried again, and every week we got closer and closer. Of course, not every recipe was a win, nor did each one make it into the final book, but with each small victory—a flavor perfected or a dish that Chip and the kids were suddenly asking for every night—a quiet confidence grew in me. And, gradually, that confidence began to drum louder than any self-doubt. In the end, we developed an entire book of recipes that now feel just as familiar and special as the ones I grew up with. Because that's what food does. We get to know it and it changes us, for better or worse. We try, we taste, then we toss away or we fall in love. That's how unfamiliar ingredients become pantry staples and new recipes become family favorites.

In my first cookbook, I shared that food is my family's love language, and through the process of putting together this one, I've grown to realize that this is likely true for all of us. Food is the musical soundtrack of our lives; it bolsters our traditions; it maintains our fondest memories and our notion of home and family and, in the most basic sense, our ability to live and breathe day in and day out. It is around food that we gather in joy and in grief; it is an offering that comforts us in bad times and enriches the good times. No other thing in the living world nourishes us physically while also affecting us on an emotional level the same way that food does. All I'm really hoping to convey is that food matters. It's an honor and a privilege to feed the people in our lives, and to gather around a table where there is always, *always* home to be found.

The Art of Gathering

I love to eat; but my absolute favorite purpose of food is that it gives us a reason to gather. Call it entertaining, call it hosting, call it dinner at seven and bring whoever you want. A gathering of any kind is time well spent, whether it's a simple meal around the kitchen table, a casual get-together, or a boisterous house full of family and friends.

The Art of Gathering

The initial intention of these beginning pages was to create somewhat of a guide to entertaining. I worked and worked on it, jotting down a few tips I'd learned over the years, but there was something about listing out rules and how-tos on a topic that can be so personal and vulnerable that just didn't feel right to me. As I thought more deeply about what exactly I'd want to convey, I realized that my heart for gathering has little to do with *how* I actually pull it off and everything to do with *why* it matters.

So, this isn't a hosting how-to. There won't be a takeaway of my top ten tips for throwing a party your friends will never forget. Nor will you learn a trick for remembering which side of the plate to put the fork on. Because in all transparency, I still have to google that myself on evenings when I feel like it matters, which isn't often. Instead, I want these pages to be an encouragement, a gracious reminder that the most valuable thing you can do when it comes to gathering, whether it's an intimate meal with your family, a last-minute dinner with friends, or an event with guests, is to free yourself from the burden of expectations. And to lean into all the life and goodness and beauty that awaits at our dinner tables.

I think it's part of our human nature to seek connection. I believe that our hearts are naturally drawn toward one another to be in community. But I've also come to realize that it's not uncommon for people to feel immobilized when it comes to inviting people into their homes. I can understand why. It's a vulnerable thing to share our most intimate spaces with others. And sure, some people may have a knack for hosting and setting a table beautifully, so it can be really easy to look wistfully at the spaces we see in magazines or on social media and feel defeated that ours will never compare. We can get so bogged down by these comparisons that we forget the beautiful simplicity of sharing a meal and swapping stories.

This is a lesson I had to learn the hard way and have continued to relearn over the years. When our kids were young and I was in a season of seeking perfection for just about every area of my life—as a wife, a mom, a designer, and a cook—whenever we'd host a dinner party or family gathering in our home, it became a rhythm for the evenings to end with me feeling completely depleted from cooking, hosting, and then stressing over how it all turned out. I never let myself indulge in the part that was meant to fill me up because I was too busy staring at the placement of the platters on the table, evaluating which ones needed fixing. I grew tired of feeling like my intentions weren't aligning. There was something in me that cared deeply about creating a space where people could feel at ease and at home within our walls, yet when the doorbell would ring I suddenly started piling on expectations that everything go perfectly.

Thankfully, there was a moment after one of our family get-togethers when I finally asked myself, "Why am I doing this?" If the answer was for my own pride or the approval of others, I knew it wasn't sustainable. There'd be no escaping that nagging feeling that I was falling short somewhere. So I started placing more significance on the why than the how and I began to anticipate simple weeknight dinners with my family in the same way I would a more elaborate gathering—for the simple sake of a mutually shared experience around the table, as well as for the significance I found in nourishing and being nourished.

Since then, meals in our home have looked and felt different for every kind of occasion. When it comes to simple weeknight dinners at home, it can sometimes feel like a victory in and of itself just to get dinner on the table for seven people after a full day of work, school, and the kids' practices. Sometimes it's fun to make dinner feel like a celebration. Even if I'm cooking something fairly simple like pasta, I'll light a few candlesticks on the table and lay out pretty linen napkins. Just those two really simple details is enough to make the meal feel a little bit more special, no matter what's being served.

On weekends, it's not uncommon for a friend or relative to stop by for a few hours and then, suddenly, it's dinnertime. It's important to me that people feel welcome to stay as long as they're comfortable—and to never feel like they're intruding on a meal they weren't invited to. So I've learned to keep on-hand ingredients for a handful of recipes that can feed a group. And I'm always up for a balanced meal of takeout and homemade. Perhaps it makes more sense to order out for a last-minute dinner while I make something sweet for dessert. When that's the case, Chip orders a pizza and I know I have the ingredients for at least three different kinds of cookies or cakes stocked in the pantry.

When I look back on some of the dinner parties and family gatherings we hosted early in our marriage, I can't help but wonder if our guests truly felt comfortable in our home. I can imagine it wasn't hard to see the anxiety written all over me. And over the years, I've watched and witnessed how my own demeanor, even the way I greet a guest in our entryway, can either set someone at ease or cause them to put up their guard.

Nowadays, when I've intentionally invited guests over for dinner, I know that the way my home feels and what it's communicating to people when they walk in is more important than what's on the menu. I've let go of the idea that the couch and pillows need to be spruced or that the floors need to be vacuumed, and instead choose to focus my time and energy on ways to make the environment feel inviting, like playing music, lighting a candle in the background, and turning on a few low lights; really anything that makes my home feel like a warm respite from the outside world and familiar enough that people want to settle in and stay awhile.

For me, the art of gathering isn't about appearance or aesthetics. It's about the way people feel when they're in my home and around my table. Whether it's my own kids or new friends, I want them to leave at the end of the night with light hearts and full stomachs. Not just from the food we shared but from the time well spent in each other's company.

Guide to Herbs, Seasonings & Substitutions

The reality is, we all need food. We can't survive without it, and I've never met anyone who'd want to. Because food fuels and satisfies. We wake up hungry for a morning meal because it breaks our fast and fills us up. We anticipate dinner because it gathers us at evening's end and declares another day done. Aside from its sustaining power, food is also creative work. Individual ingredients come together to create something distinctly delicious—especially in the form of fresh herbs and flavorful seasonings.

Fresh Herbs

This guide features some of the most common herbs available in supermarkets and farmers' markets. You can use this to get an idea of their flavors and the best ways to use them.

Italian basil
FLAVOR: *anise, cloves, mint*

USES: *pasta sauce, pesto, salad*

dill
FLAVOR: *grassy, mild*

USES: *eggs, fish, poultry, vegetables*

rosemary
FLAVOR: *aromatic, piney*

USES: *apples, pears, potatoes, red meat, stuffing*

bay laurel
FLAVOR: *aromatic, vanilla, cardamom*

USES: *beans, braised meat, poultry, soup, stew*

mint
FLAVOR: *menthol, icy, zesty*

USES: *cocktails, lamb, salads, tea*

sage
FLAVOR: *smoky, woodsy*

USES: *meat, poultry, sausage, stuffing*

chives
FLAVOR: *oniony*

USES: *dips, eggs, vegetables*

oregano
FLAVOR: *anise, cloves, mint*

USES: *chili, grilled or roasted meat, pasta sauce*

tarragon
FLAVOR: *anise, exotic, sweet*

USES: *asparagus, béarnaise sauce, fish, peas, poultry*

cilantro
FLAVOR: *citrus, pungent*

USES: *marinades, Mexican and Thai dishes, salsa*

parsley
FLAVOR: *bitter*

USES: *most meats and vegetables*

thyme
FLAVOR: *earthy, fragrant, mild lemon*

USES: *meat, poultry, sauces, broth, vegetables*

Herb Pairings

Fresh herbs are perfect on their own, but mixing and matching them produces comforting combos and sometimes even unexpectedly wonderful results. Whether you are clipping from a garden or pot or you have bounty from the market, give these combinations a try.

HERBS	PAIRING SUGGESTION
cilantro & dill	Add dill to dishes that use fresh cilantro—think Mexican and Thai—for a subtle but distinct shift in flavor.
dill & chives	Stir this pair into a cold chicken salad or egg salad, toss with lightly sautéed summer vegetables, or top sliced fresh tomatoes.
mint, oregano & parsley	Parsley marries the distinct flavors of mint and oregano to add a Mediterranean or Middle Eastern take on grain salads and marinades for grilled meats.
parsley, rosemary & thyme	These herbs create a classic comfort-food combo. Use them with roasted or braised meat or chicken (rub it under the skin), in stuffing, and with roasted vegetables.
sage & parsley	With their warm blend of flavors, this duo works with creamy risotto, roasted winter squash, stuffing, and roasted or braised meats.
thyme & tarragon	This combo goes best with mild foods. Stir them into a sour cream or mustard sauce to spoon over fish and fresh spring vegetables. Or toss them chopped into scrambled eggs or omelets.
basil & thyme	Add these reliable herbs to tomato-based sauces, eggplant dishes (ratatouille or caponata), quiche, and fresh salads.
basil & mint	Use equal amounts of each herb to make pesto to drizzle over tomatoes, toss with pasta, or whisk into a vinaigrette dressing. Or sprinkle this chopped herb combo over a plate of sliced mixed melon for a refreshing salad.

Seasoning Blends

Making your own spice blends produces the freshest flavors in recipes and allows you to adjust seasoning levels to your personal preference. These formulas all make about ¼ cup. Once prepared, store them in small glass jars in your pantry for up to 1 year.

apple pie spice

2 tablespoons ground cinnamon

1 tablespoon ground nutmeg

1 teaspoon ground ginger

½ teaspoon ground cloves

Use to season apple pie and other baked goods. Add to French toast and pancakes. Sprinkle on yogurt and blend into smoothies.

chai spice

4 teaspoons ground cardamom

2 teaspoons ground cinnamon

2 teaspoons ground ginger

1 teaspoon ground allspice

1 teaspoon ground nutmeg

½ teaspoon anise seeds, ground

½ teaspoon ground cloves

Steep a spoonful with your tea or blend into a smoothie. Stir into hot oatmeal. Add to banana bread batter.

pumpkin pie spice

2 tablespoons ground cinnamon

1 tablespoon ground ginger

2 teaspoons ground nutmeg

1 teaspoon ground allspice

½ teaspoon ground cloves

Use in pumpkin or sweet potato pie. Add to a latte or whipped cream.

Cajun seasoning

1 tablespoon sweet paprika

2 teaspoons garlic powder

1½ teaspoons dried oregano

1 teaspoon onion powder

1 teaspoon black pepper

1 teaspoon kosher salt

½ to 1 teaspoon cayenne pepper

½ teaspoon dried thyme

½ teaspoon white pepper

Use in Cajun and Creole dishes, such as jambalaya. Season shrimp skewers, crab cakes, and fish. Sprinkle on popcorn or your favorite snack mix.

Greek seasoning

5 teaspoons dried oregano

1 tablespoon dried thyme

2 teaspoons dried marjoram

2 teaspoons dried minced onion

1 teaspoon dried basil

1 teaspoon dried minced garlic

1 teaspoon dried lemon peel

1 teaspoon kosher salt

Season chicken thighs and pork tenderloin. Stir into orzo with tomatoes and feta. Sprinkle over salads or add to vinaigrette.

Italian seasoning

1 tablespoon dried basil

1 tablespoon dried oregano

1 tablespoon dried thyme

1½ teaspoons dried marjoram

1½ teaspoons dried rosemary

½ teaspoon crushed red pepper flakes (optional)

Add to pasta sauces, meatballs, soups, salad dressings, and roasted vegetables.

Southwest seasoning

1 tablespoon ground ancho chile

1 tablespoon sweet paprika

1½ teaspoons dried Mexican oregano

1½ teaspoons onion powder

1 teaspoon ground chipotle

1 teaspoon garlic powder

1 teaspoon ground coriander

½ teaspoon ground cumin

½ teaspoon kosher salt

Season grilled meats. Stir into rice and bean blends or sautéed vegetables. Add to scrambled eggs.

poultry seasoning

1 tablespoon dried sage

1 tablespoon dried thyme

2 teaspoons dried marjoram

1 teaspoon dried rosemary

1 teaspoon kosher salt

½ teaspoon dried dill weed

½ teaspoon dried lemon peel

½ teaspoon black pepper

¼ teaspoon ground allspice

Rub under the skin of roast chicken and turkey. Stir into stuffing and soups. Work into ground chicken to make burgers.

steak seasoning

4 teaspoons kosher salt

1 tablespoon cracked black pepper

2 teaspoons dried minced garlic

1½ teaspoons dill seeds

1 teaspoon onion powder

1 teaspoon smoked paprika

1 teaspoon dried lemon peel

Sprinkle on steaks and pot roast. Stir into stews. Toss with vegetables.

barbecue seasoning

5 teaspoons chili powder

1 tablespoon smoked paprika

2 teaspoons mustard powder

2 teaspoons dried minced onion

½ teaspoon garlic powder

½ teaspoon kosher salt

½ teaspoon black pepper

Rub on ribs and chicken. Sprinkle over roasted vegetables. Stir into baked beans and sauces.

chili seasoning

2 tablespoons chili powder

2 teaspoons unsweetened cocoa powder

2 teaspoons dried minced onion

1 teaspoon dried Mexican oregano

1 teaspoon ground cumin

½ teaspoon ground cinnamon

½ teaspoon garlic powder

½ teaspoon kosher salt

½ teaspoon black pepper

Add to your favorite chili or baked beans. Sprinkle on oven fries.

fajita seasoning

1 tablespoon chili powder

2 teaspoons sweet paprika

2 teaspoons dried Mexican oregano

1½ teaspoons onion powder

1 teaspoon garlic powder

1 teaspoon kosher salt

½ teaspoon ground cumin

¼ teaspoon black pepper

¼ teaspoon cayenne pepper

Rub on chicken, beef, shrimp,and pork. Stir into black beans or rice.

lemon-pepper seasoning

2 tablespoons dried lemon peel

1 tablespoon cracked black pepper

1 teaspoon kosher salt

1 teaspoon onion powder

Sprinkle over salmon and chicken. Season popcorn and snack mixes. Add to marinades.

pizza seasoning

1 tablespoon dried basil

1 tablespoon dried oregano

2 teaspoons dried parsley

1½ teaspoons dried minced garlic

1½ teaspoons fennel seeds

1½ teaspoons dried minced onion

¼ teaspoon crushed red pepper flakes

Sprinkle over homemade or store-bought pizza.

taco seasoning

1 tablespoon chili powder

2½ teaspoons ground cumin

2 teaspoons sugar

1 teaspoon garlic powder

1 teaspoon kosher salt

½ teaspoon dried Mexican oregano

½ teaspoon black pepper

¼ teaspoon crushed red pepper flakes (optional)

Stir into ground meat with water to make taco meat. Sprinkle over chicken, shrimp, or fish. Stir into sour cream for an easy dip.

everything bagel seasoning

4 teaspoons poppy seeds

2 teaspoons toasted sesame seeds

2 teaspoons dried minced garlic

2 teaspoons dried minced onion

1½ teaspoons kosher salt

Top bagels with lox and cream cheese. Sprinkle on eggs, avocado, and tomatoes.

Substitutions

When you find yourself in the middle of a recipe and discover you're missing a key ingredient, check here to see if you can save yourself a trip to the store.

INGREDIENT	SUBSTITUTE WITH
baking powder *1 teaspoon*	½ teaspoon cream of tartar + ½ teaspoon baking soda
balsamic vinegar *1 tablespoon*	1 tablespoon red wine vinegar + ½ teaspoon brown sugar
bread crumbs, *fine dried* *¼ cup*	¾ cup soft bread crumbs (1 slice of bread)
broth *beef, chicken, or vegetable* *1 cup*	1 teaspoon broth base or bouillon granules + 1 cup hot water
buttermilk *1 cup*	1 tablespoon vinegar or lemon juice + enough milk to make 1 cup (stir and let stand 5 minutes)
cornstarch *(for thickening)* *1 tablespoon*	2 tablespoons all-purpose flour
corn syrup *(light)* *1 cup*	1 cup granulated sugar + ¼ cup hot water
crème fraîche *1 cup*	1 cup sour cream or plain Greek yogurt
egg *1 whole*	¼ cup refrigerated or frozen egg product; or, for baking, 1 tablespoon flaxseed + 3 tablespoons water (beat together and let stand for 5 minutes)
flour, *cake* *1 cup*	1 cup minus 2 tablespoons all-purpose flour, sifted
flour, *self-rising* *1 cup*	1 cup all-purpose flour + 1 teaspoon baking powder + ½ teaspoon kosher salt + ¼ teaspoon baking soda
garlic *1 clove*	½ teaspoon bottled minced garlic or garlic paste, or ⅛ teaspoon garlic powder

ginger, *grated fresh* *1 teaspoon*	¼ teaspoon ground ginger
half-and-half or light cream *1 cup*	1 tablespoon melted butter + enough whole milk to make 1 cup
lemon juice *1 tablespoon*	1½ teaspoons apple cider vinegar or white wine vinegar
milk *1 cup*	1 cup plant milk (unsweetened, unflavored plant milk, such as almond, cashew, oat, soy)
mustard powder *1 teaspoon*	1 tablespoon yellow mustard (in cooking)
onion, *chopped* *½ cup*	½ cup chopped green onions or shallots, or 2 tablespoons dried minced onion
sour cream *1 cup*	1 cup plain Greek yogurt or regular yogurt
sugar, *brown* *1 cup packed*	1 cup granulated sugar + 2 tablespoons molasses
sugar, *granulated* *1 cup*	1 cup packed brown sugar, or 2 cups sifted powdered sugar
tomato sauce *1 cup*	½ cup tomato paste + ½ cup water
vanilla bean *1 whole*	1 tablespoon vanilla bean paste or pure vanilla extract
wine, *red* *1 cup*	1 cup broth (beef, chicken, or vegetable) in savory recipes, or 1 cup 100% cranberry juice (for baked recipes)
wine, *white* *1 cup*	1 cup chicken broth in savory recipes, or 1 cup apple juice in desserts
yogurt *1 cup plain*	1 cup plain Greek yogurt or 1 cup sour cream

CHAPTER ONE

Scratch Made

THE REWARD IS IN WHAT GETS

CREATED ALONG THE WAY

Homemade Pie Crust

prep: *20 minutes,*
plus 2 hours chilling

cook: *under 25 minutes,*
if blind baking

cool: *as directed in*
the pie recipe

1¼ cups all-purpose flour, plus more for rolling

1 teaspoon kosher salt

8 tablespoons (1 stick) unsalted butter, cut into ½-inch cubes and chilled

¼ cup ice-cold water

1 large egg (if blind baking)

1. To make by hand: In a large bowl, whisk together the flour and salt. Scatter in the butter and use a pastry blender or your fingers to cut the butter into the flour until the biggest pieces are the size of small peas. Gradually drizzle the water on top, using a rubber spatula or your hands to stir until the dough comes together. The dough should not be watery or wet.

2. To make in a food processor: Pulse together the flour and salt. Sprinkle the butter over the flour and pulse until the butter is coated in flour and the biggest pieces are the size of small peas. Drizzle the water on top and pulse until the dough comes together. The dough should not be watery or wet.

3. Shape the dough into a flattened ball. Wrap it tightly in plastic wrap and refrigerate for at least 1 hour. (The dough can be tightly wrapped and frozen for up to 1 month at this point. Thaw in the refrigerator before proceeding.)

4. Lightly dust the counter with flour and roll the dough out to a round 2½ inches larger than a 9-inch pie plate or 3½ inches larger than a 9-inch deep-dish pie plate. Transfer the dough to the pie plate and carefully ease it into the edges. Trim the dough to an even ½ inch all around and fold it under itself on top of the rim. Use your fingers to crimp the crust along the rim. Refrigerate for 1 hour. If the pie or quiche recipe calls for an unbaked crust, you're ready to go ahead with that recipe.

5. If your recipe calls for a blind-baked crust, preheat the oven to 425°F and proceed to step 6.

6. Use a fork to poke the dough several times on the bottom and sides of the pie plate (this is called docking). Line the chilled dough with parchment paper or foil. Fill with dried beans or pie weights, gently spreading them so that they cover the full base and the edges.

7. Bake until the edges of the dough are just beginning to brown, about 15 minutes. Remove the crust from the oven and carefully transfer the parchment or foil with the beans or weights to a large heatproof bowl. Return the crust to the oven and bake until the bottom is dry and lightly browned, about 5 minutes. Beat the egg with 1 tablespoon water in a small dish. Gently brush the egg over the bottom of the crust. Bake for 1 minute to cook the egg.

8. Let cool or proceed as directed in the recipe.

Makes one 9-inch regular or deep-dish crust

Graham Cracker Crust

prep: *10 minutes*   **cook:** *under 10 minutes*   **cool:** *30 minutes*

1½ cups graham cracker crumbs

⅓ cup sugar

6 tablespoons (¾ stick) unsalted butter, melted

1. Preheat the oven to 350°F.

2. In a large bowl, combine the graham cracker crumbs and sugar. Stir to blend. Stir in the melted butter until well blended.

3. Press the mixture into the bottom and up the sides of a 9-inch deep-dish pie plate.

4. Bake until firm, about 8 minutes. Let cool completely before filling.

Makes one 9-inch deep-dish crust

Tart Shell

prep: *25 minutes, plus 1 hour 30 minutes chilling*   **cook:** *30 minutes*   **cool:** *30 minutes*

1¼ cups all-purpose flour, plus more for rolling

½ cup powdered sugar

½ teaspoon kosher salt

8 tablespoons (1 stick) cold unsalted butter, cubed

1 large egg

½ teaspoon pure vanilla extract

1. In a stand mixer fitted with the paddle attachment, whisk together the flour, powdered sugar, and salt until fully combined. Add the cold butter and mix until the dough is crumbly and the butter resembles small peas. Scrape the sides and bottom of the bowl if needed. Add the egg and vanilla and mix just until fully combined. Be sure not to overmix or the dough will be tough. The dough should stick together when pressed without feeling dry or crumbly.

2. Turn the dough onto a lightly floured surface and form into a ball; it should come together easily without being sticky. Flatten the ball slightly with your hands to form a thick disk. Wrap with plastic wrap and refrigerate for at least 1 hour.

3. Take the dough out of the fridge and let it sit on the counter for a few minutes to soften slightly for easy rolling. On a lightly floured surface, roll the dough out into an 11-inch round ¼ inch thick. Place gently into a 9-inch tart pan, preferably with a removable bottom. You can do this by flouring a rolling pin and rolling the dough loosely around it, then unrolling it into the pan and easing it into the edges. Brush away any excess flour on the surface. With a sharp knife, trim the edges of the pastry to fit the tart pan. Cover the pan with plastic wrap and place in the freezer until firm, about 30 minutes. (Frozen dough is less prone to shrinking while baking.)

4. If the recipe calls for an unbaked crust, you're ready to go ahead. If it calls for a blind-baked crust, position a rack in the middle of the oven and preheat the oven to 375°F.

5. Lay a sheet of parchment paper or foil over the tart crust, fitting it into the bottom of the pan and covering the edges of the crust to keep it from burning. Fill the bottom of the tart pan with pie weights, dried beans, or uncooked rice, making sure they're distributed over the entire surface.

6. Bake the crust until the parchment or foil no longer sticks to the dough, about 20 minutes. Transfer the crust to a wire rack and remove the pie weights and parchment or foil. Return the crust to the oven and bake until golden brown and dry, about 10 minutes longer. Transfer to a wire rack and let cool completely, about 30 minutes.

7. Proceed with filling the tart shell according to the recipe.

Makes one 9-inch tart shell

Homemade Pizza Dough

prep: *1 hour 30 minutes*   **cook:** *under 15 minutes*   **cool:** *none*

1¼ teaspoons active dry yeast

½ teaspoon sugar

¼ cup warm water (95° to
   110°F)

3½ cups bread flour

2 teaspoons kosher salt

¼ cup olive oil

1 cup plus 1 tablespoon room-
   temperature water

Cooking spray

1. In a small bowl, stir together the yeast, sugar, and warm water. Let stand until foamy, about 5 minutes.

2. Add the flour to the bowl of a stand mixer fitted with the dough hook. Sprinkle the salt over the flour and mix on low speed for 15 seconds to distribute the salt.

3. Add the olive oil, room-temperature water, and yeast mixture and mix on low speed for 1 to 2 minutes, then increase the speed to medium and mix until a ball of dough forms, about 5 minutes.

4. Spray a medium bowl lightly with cooking spray. Shape the dough into a ball and set it in the bowl seam side down. Cover the bowl with plastic wrap and place in a warm area until doubled in size, about 1 hour.

5. When the dough is almost risen, place a cast-iron pizza stone on the center rack of the oven and preheat the oven to 500°F.

6. When the dough has risen, remove the plastic wrap and push down on the dough to release the gases and bubbles. Shape it into a ball. (If using the dough later, cover with plastic wrap and place in the refrigerator for up to 12 hours. The dough will slowly proof during that time. Once you're ready to use it, set it out for 30 minutes to come to room temperature.)

7. Spread a piece of parchment paper about 1½ feet long on a work surface. Stretch the dough into a 14-inch round on the parchment.

8. Top with your favorite toppings (or see the recipes on pages 219 to 221). Carefully pull the oven rack with the pizza stone halfway out of the oven and transfer the parchment and pizza dough to the stone.

9. Bake until the crust is golden, 13 to 15 minutes. Transfer the pizza to a cutting board and cut into 8 slices to serve.

Makes enough dough for one 14-inch pizza

Homemade Tortillas

prep: *15 minutes for corn,*   **cook:** *under 20 minutes for corn,*   **cool:** *none*
55 minutes for flour   *under 10 minutes for flour*

corn tortillas

1½ cups masa harina

½ teaspoon kosher salt

1 cup hot water (170° to
190°F)

flour tortillas

3 cups all-purpose flour,
plus more for rolling

1 teaspoon kosher salt

1½ teaspoons baking powder

⅓ cup vegetable shortening

1 cup hot water (105° to
110°F)

to make the corn tortillas

1. In a large bowl, stir together the masa harina and salt, then add the hot water. Knead the dough in the bowl until it has the consistency of Play-Doh. If the dough cracks when squeezed, it is too dry; add a tablespoon or two of water until you reach the right consistency. Cover with plastic wrap.

2. Heat a large cast-iron skillet over medium heat. Line a tortilla press with a plastic bag to prevent the dough from sticking. Line a plate with a towel.

3. Uncover the dough and pinch off 8 golf-ball-size chunks (about 1¾ ounces each). Roll them into balls and flatten them in the press to create 6-inch rounds.

4. Place one tortilla in the hot skillet. Cook 30 seconds, flip with a spatula or tongs, cook another 30 seconds, and flip again. Cook until the tortilla slightly puffs up, about 30 seconds more. Transfer the tortilla to the towel-lined plate and cover with a paper towel. Repeat with the remaining tortillas.

to make the flour tortillas

1. In a stand mixer fitted with the dough hook, beat the flour, salt, and baking powder on low speed until combined, about 10 seconds. Add the shortening and beat on medium until the mixture resembles coarse crumbs, about 1 minute. With the mixer still running, slowly pour in the hot water and beat until the dough starts to come together and become sticky, about 40 seconds, scraping down the sides of the bowl as needed. Transfer to a lightly floured work surface and shape into a smooth ball.

2. Return the dough ball to the mixer bowl and cover with a clean kitchen towel. Let stand at room temperature for 45 minutes. (The dough will not increase in size.) Cut the dough into 10 pieces (about 2 ounces each).

3. Heat a large cast-iron skillet over high heat until smoking, then reduce the heat to medium. Working with one piece of dough at a time, roll it out on a lightly floured surface to a thin 7½- to 8-inch round. Transfer to the hot skillet and cook until pliable and lightly browned in spots, 30 to 40 seconds per side. Transfer to a towel-lined plate and cover with a paper towel.

Makes 8 corn tortillas and 10 flour tortillas

Homemade Noodles

prep: *30 minutes*   **cook:** *under 20 minutes*   **cool:** *none*

Boxed pasta is certainly a staple in my pantry and something I rely on often, especially during busy weeknights; however, it's true that nothing quite compares to the real deal. Anything made from scratch feels like creative work to me. I pull this homemade noodle recipe out for special occasions. It elevates the dish in a way the boxed stuff can't, and has become a favorite of the kids to help me make. It's always then, with our sleeves rolled up and spreading out the dough, that I'm reminded that the reward of homemade is not only in the taste, but in the time spent getting to create along the way.

2½ cups all-purpose flour,
    plus more as needed

2 large eggs

½ cup milk, plus more as
    needed

½ teaspoon kosher salt

1. Place the flour in a large bowl or on a clean work surface and make a well in the center. Crack the eggs into the well. Add the milk and salt and mix with a fork until the dough comes together. Knead to incorporate all the flour. (Add a little more flour if the dough is too sticky. Add more milk if too dry.)

2. On a lightly floured surface, use a rolling pin to roll out the dough into a round that is about ⅛ inch thick. It does not need to be perfect. Using a knife or pizza cutter, cut the dough into strips about 1 inch wide and 5 to 6 inches long. (Again, they don't have to be perfectly even.)

3. Cover with a damp paper towel to avoid them drying out. Let the dough rest for about 15 minutes.

4. Add the noodles to boiling water or other cooking liquid as specified by the recipe you're using and let simmer until the noodles are tender, 10 to 15 minutes.

Makes 1 pound of noodles, to serve 6 to 8 people

TIP: *These noodles should be cooked the same day they're made.*

Homemade Gnocchi

prep: *2 hours*   **cook:** *under 20 minutes*   **cool:** *none*

½ cup plus 1 teaspoon kosher salt

2½ pounds russet potatoes (about 4)

2 large eggs, lightly beaten

1 large egg yolk, lightly beaten

2½ cups all-purpose flour, plus more for rolling

2 tablespoons canola oil

Choice of sauce: see pairings on pages 36 and 37

1. Preheat the oven to 400°F.

2. Spread the ½ cup salt on a sheet pan, creating a salt bed.

3. Using a fork, poke each potato all over to allow for steam to vent. Place the potatoes along the salt bed, keeping equal distance between the potatoes (a). Bake until tender when pierced with a paring knife, about 1 hour 15 minutes.

4. Carefully halve the potatoes lengthwise and scoop the insides into a bowl to cool, about 15 minutes (b). Press the insides of the potatoes through a potato ricer into a large bowl (c). Set aside until cool enough to work with.

5. Create a well on a flat surface. Crack eggs into the center and mix with the potatoes (d). Working quickly, sprinkle the flour and the remaining 1 teaspoon salt over the potatoes and gently fold in the flour and salt. Turn the dough out onto a lightly floured surface and gently knead just until the dough comes together. Divide the dough into 8 equal portions and cover with a clean kitchen towel.

6. Working with one portion of dough at a time, use your hands to roll the dough back and forth while moving them outward to elongate the dough into a ¾-inch-diameter rope. Using a dough scraper or knife, cut the rope into 1- to 2-inch pieces (e).

7. Bring a large pot of salted water to a boil over high heat. Line a sheet pan with a clean kitchen towel. Working in 3 or 4 batches (so the gnocchi have plenty of room to cook), gently add the gnocchi to the simmering water. (Be sure to let the water return to a simmer between batches.) When they rise to the surface, cook until slightly firm, about 1 minute (f). Using a spider or slotted spoon, transfer the gnocchi to the towel-lined sheet pan. Let cool for 10 minutes.

8. In a large nonstick skillet, heat 1 tablespoon of the canola oil over medium-high heat. Add half of the gnocchi. Cook, stirring occasionally, until golden brown, 4 to 6 minutes. Transfer to a plate and repeat with the remaining canola oil and gnocchi. Return the browned gnocchi to the skillet and toss with the sauce of your choice.

Makes 4 servings

TIP: *You can freeze the gnocchi after step 6 to save for quick dinners. If cooking from frozen, start with step 7. When gnocchi rise to the surface, cook until slightly firm, about 5 minutes.*

a

b

c

d

e

f

Jo's Marinara Sauce

prep: *15 minutes*   **cook:** *under 40 minutes*   **cool:** *none*

1 tablespoon olive oil

⅓ cup diced red onion (about ½ small)

2 garlic cloves, minced

1 teaspoon kosher salt, plus more to taste

1 teaspoon freshly ground black pepper, plus more to taste

One 28-ounce can crushed tomatoes

One 6-ounce can tomato paste

3 bay leaves

2 tablespoons chopped fresh basil

1 tablespoon chopped fresh parsley

1 teaspoon dried oregano

1. In a large pot, heat the olive oil over medium heat. Add the onion and sauté until translucent and browning, 8 to 10 minutes.

2. Add the garlic, salt, and pepper and cook for 1 minute, stirring occasionally. Add the tomatoes, tomato paste, and 2 cups water. Stir well to combine. Stir in the bay leaves, basil, parsley, and oregano. Reduce the heat to low and simmer, stirring occasionally, until thick, 20 to 30 minutes.

3. Remove and discard the bay leaves. Season the sauce with salt and pepper to taste.

4. Serve immediately, or let cool and store in an airtight container in the fridge for up to 3 days or in the freezer for up to 1 month.

Makes about 5 cups

Brown Sage Butter

prep: *5 minutes*   **cook:** *under 5 minutes*   **cool:** *none*

4 tablespoons (½ stick) unsalted butter

16 to 20 fresh sage leaves

Kosher salt and freshly ground black pepper

In a small skillet, heat the butter until it begins to brown, 2 to 3 minutes. Add the sage leaves and let them fry slightly in the butter, 1 to 2 minutes. Don't let them burn! Season with salt and pepper and serve immediately.

Makes ½ cup

Pesto

prep: *10 minutes*   **cook:** *none*   **cool:** *none*

3 cups packed fresh basil leaves

2 garlic cloves

¼ cup pine nuts

¾ cup extra virgin olive oil

½ cup grated Parmesan cheese (about 2 ounces)

¼ teaspoon kosher salt

¼ teaspoon freshly ground black pepper

1. In a food processor, combine the basil, garlic, and pine nuts. Pulse until roughly chopped, 10 to 15 seconds.

2. With the machine running, slowly drizzle in the olive oil until well combined, 1 to 2 minutes.

3. Add the Parmesan, salt, and pepper and mix until just incorporated.

4. Serve immediately, or store in an airtight container in the refrigerator for up to 3 days or in the freezer for up to 1 month.

Makes about 1½ cups

gnocchi sauce pairings

GNOCCHI AND MARINARA: After browning the gnocchi, return both batches to the skillet, add ⅓ cup Jo's Marinara Sauce (opposite), and toss to coat. Sprinkle with ¼ cup grated Parmesan cheese and 1 tablespoon torn fresh basil and serve.

GNOCCHI AND BROWN SAGE BUTTER: After browning the gnocchi, use the same skillet to start the Brown Sage Butter (opposite), then add both batches of the browned gnocchi when you add the sage leaves. Stir and toss to coat. Season with salt and pepper to taste and serve.

GNOCCHI AND PESTO: After browning the gnocchi, return both batches to the skillet, add ⅓ cup Pesto (above), and toss to coat. Sprinkle with ¼ cup grated Parmesan cheese and serve.

CHAPTER TWO

Breads

AN AGE-OLD ART FORM THAT

BECKONS OUR SENSES BACK TO A

FAMILIAR PLACE TIME AND AGAIN

Garlic Knots

prep: *3 hours 25 minutes*   **cook:** *under 15 minutes*   **cool:** *none*

These are classic garlic rolls that I shape into a knot for a more elevated dish. It's a fun baking process to include the kids in—they love to help form the dough into knots (some take more creative liberty than others) and watch how they rise in the oven. I typically serve these with pasta—I just love the way the garlic flavors meld with a creamy sauce.

dough

¾ cup warm water (95° to 110°F)

1 teaspoon sugar

One ¼-ounce packet active dry yeast

2¼ cups bread flour, plus more for the work surface

1 teaspoon kosher salt

2 tablespoons olive oil, plus more for oiling the bowl

garlic topping

5 tablespoons unsalted butter

4 garlic cloves, minced

2 tablespoons minced fresh parsley

1 teaspoon flaky sea salt, such as Maldon

1. To make the dough: In a small bowl, combine the warm water, sugar, and yeast. Let sit for about 5 minutes, until the sugar and yeast are dissolved.

2. In a stand mixer fitted with the dough hook, combine the bread flour and salt. Add the yeast mixture and 1 tablespoon of the olive oil and mix on medium-low speed for about 5 minutes, until the dough is a little sticky but pulls away from the bowl.

3. Shape the dough into a ball. Place in a bowl well coated with olive oil and cover with plastic wrap. Let rise in a warm spot until doubled in size, 1 hour 30 minutes to 1 hour 50 minutes (or refrigerate overnight for a slow rise).

4. Line two baking sheets with parchment paper.

5. Uncover the bowl and punch down the dough to release the air. On a surface sprinkled with flour, divide the dough into quarters. Work with one portion at a time, covering the remaining portions with plastic wrap or a damp towel. Divide each portion into quarters and roll each until 6 to 7 inches long. Tie into a knot and place on the prepared pans. Repeat to make 16 total knots, leaving 2 inches between the knots.

6. Brush the knots with the remaining 1 tablespoon olive oil and cover with plastic wrap or a damp towel. Let rise until doubled in size, about 1 hour.

7. Meanwhile, preheat the oven to 400°F.

8. Transfer the pans to the oven and bake until the knots are golden brown on the top, 12 to 15 minutes.

9. Meanwhile, to make the garlic topping: in a small saucepan, melt the butter. Add the garlic and swirl until fragrant, then remove from the heat. Add the parsley and stir to combine. As soon as the knots come out of the oven, brush the tops with the garlic butter. Sprinkle with the sea salt and serve warm.

10. Store in a zip-top bag or airtight container at room temperature for up to 3 days.

Makes 16 knots

Focaccia

prep: *2 hours 25 minutes*   **cook:** *under 25 minutes*   **cool:** *under 10 minutes*

dough

1¾ cups warm water (95° to 110°F)

One ¼-ounce packet active dry yeast

3 teaspoons sugar

5 cups bread flour

1 tablespoon kosher salt

½ cup plus 2 tablespoons olive oil

Cooking spray

topping

3 tablespoons olive oil

1 tablespoon coarse sea salt

1 tablespoon fresh rosemary

1. To make the dough: In a small bowl, combine ¼ cup of the warm water, the yeast, and 1 teaspoon of the sugar. Let stand until foamy, about 5 minutes.

2. In a stand mixer fitted with the dough hook, combine the flour and kosher salt. With the mixer on low speed, slowly pour in the yeast mixture, the remaining 1½ cups of warm water, ½ cup of the olive oil, and the remaining 2 teaspoons sugar. Turn the mixer to medium-high speed and mix for 5 minutes. The dough will form a ball and pull away from the sides.

3. Spray a large bowl lightly with cooking spray and place the ball of dough in the bowl. Cover with plastic wrap and let rise in a warm spot until doubled in size, about 1 hour.

4. Drizzle the remaining 2 tablespoons olive oil onto a rimmed 17 × 13-inch sheet pan.

5. Punch down the dough to release the air. Place it on the prepared pan and press it out with lightly oiled hands to fill the pan, pushing your fingers into the dough to create small divots in it.

6. Cover the pan loosely with plastic wrap and place the dough in a warm area to rise until pillowy, about 1 hour.

7. Meanwhile, preheat the oven to 425°F.

8. To make the topping: Drizzle the top of the dough with 2 tablespoons of the olive oil, the sea salt, and rosemary.

9. Transfer the pan to the oven and bake until the top of the focaccia is golden brown, 20 to 25 minutes. Remove from the oven and drizzle with the remaining 1 tablespoon olive oil. Let cool for 5 to 10 minutes before cutting into 12 pieces.

10. Store in an airtight container at room temperature for up to 3 days.

Makes 12 servings

Dinner Rolls

prep: *1 hour 50 minutes*   **cook:** *25 minutes*   **cool:** *none*

½ cup warm water (95° to 110°F)

Two ¼-ounce packets active dry yeast

⅓ cup plus 2 teaspoons sugar

1½ cups whole milk

5½ to 6 cups all-purpose flour

1½ teaspoons kosher salt

2 large eggs

12 tablespoons (1½ sticks) unsalted butter, 1 stick at room temperature and ½ stick melted

Cooking spray

2 teaspoons Maldon salt or other flaky salt

1. In a small bowl, combine the warm water, yeast, and 2 teaspoons of the sugar. Let stand until foamy, about 5 minutes.

2. In a small saucepan, warm the milk to between 100° and 110°F.

3. In a stand mixer fitted with the dough hook, combine 5½ cups of the flour, the remaining ⅓ cup sugar, and the kosher salt. Give it a quick stir to mix the ingredients.

4. Turn the mixer on low and slowly add the yeast mixture, warmed milk, eggs, and softened butter. Mix until a smooth dough is formed, 4 to 5 minutes. The dough should be slightly sticky but able to pull away from the sides of the bowl. If the dough sticks to the bowl, add flour 1 tablespoon at a time until it reaches the desired texture.

5. Transfer the dough to a medium bowl lightly sprayed with cooking spray and cover with plastic wrap. Set in a warm spot until doubled in size, about 40 minutes.

6. Remove the plastic wrap and lightly punch down the dough to release the air.

7. Using a kitchen scale, divide and weigh the dough into 32 pieces (about 1½ ounces each). Gently roll the dough pieces into balls and place them touching on a sheet pan.

8. Loosely cover with plastic wrap and let rise at room temperature for 40 minutes, or until soft and pillowy. They should bounce back a bit if lightly touched.

9. While the dough is rising, preheat the oven to 375°F.

10. Remove the plastic wrap, transfer the rolls to the oven, and bake until deep golden brown, about 25 minutes.

11. When the rolls come out of the oven, immediately brush them with the melted butter and sprinkle with the Maldon salt. Serve warm.

12. Store in an airtight container at room temperature for up to 2 days.

Makes 32 rolls

Crostini

One 16-ounce baguette

2 tablespoons olive oil

½ teaspoon kosher salt

½ teaspoon freshly ground
    black pepper

1. Preheat the oven to 425°F. Line a baking sheet with foil.

2. Using a serrated knife, cut the baguette on the diagonal into forty-eight ½-inch-thick slices.

3. Using a pastry brush, brush one side of each slice with the olive oil. Place oil-side up on the prepared pan. Sprinkle with the salt and pepper.

4. Transfer to the oven and toast until golden brown, about 10 minutes, flipping the crostini halfway through.

5. Remove and let cool 30 minutes before serving. If making ahead, cool completely before storing.

6. Store in an airtight container at room temperature for up to 3 days.

Makes forty-eight ½-inch crostini

TIP: *Serve the crostini with any soup, eat them with dips as an alternative to chips, or use as the basis for bruschetta (page 141).*

Braided Loaf

prep: *2 hours 5 minutes*   **cook:** *under 30 minutes*   **cool:** *50 minutes*

dough

¾ cup warm water (95° to 110°F)

One ¼-ounce packet active dry yeast

3 teaspoons sugar

3½ cups all-purpose flour, plus more for the work surface

1 teaspoon kosher salt

3 tablespoons canola oil

2 large eggs

Cooking spray

topping

1 large egg

1 teaspoon heavy cream

2 teaspoons sesame seeds

1. To make the dough: In a small bowl, combine ¼ cup of the warm water, the yeast, and 1 teaspoon of the sugar. Let stand until foamy, about 5 minutes.

2. In a stand mixer fitted with the dough hook, combine the flour, remaining 2 teaspoons sugar, and the salt. With the mixer on low speed, pour in the yeast mixture, the remaining ½ cup warm water, the oil, and eggs. Mix on medium speed for 5 minutes, until the dough forms a ball and pulls away from the sides.

3. Spray a large bowl lightly with cooking spray and place the dough in the bowl. Cover with plastic wrap and let the dough rise in a warm spot until doubled in size, about 1 hour.

4. Punch down the dough to release the air. Turn out the dough onto a lightly floured surface. Divide the dough into 3 equal portions. Roll each into a ball and then into a 15-inch-long rope.

5. Spray a baking sheet with cooking spray. Place the 3 ropes parallel to one another on the pan. Starting at one end of the dough ropes, carefully braid them. Pinch the ends to seal and tuck the ends underneath the braid so that only the braid shows.

6. Lightly cover the pan with plastic wrap and let rise until pillowy, about 45 minutes.

7. Meanwhile, preheat the oven to 375°F.

8. To prepare the topping: In a small bowl, whisk together the egg and cream. Gently brush it over the dough. Sprinkle the dough with the sesame seeds.

9. Bake until golden brown, about 28 minutes. Let the loaf cool for about 10 minutes, then transfer to a wire rack to cool completely, about 40 minutes, before serving.

10. Store in a zip-top bag or airtight container at room temperature for up to 3 days.

Makes 1 loaf

TIP: *Serve slices of the bread with salted butter.*

Becki's Herb Butter

prep: *15 minutes* **cook:** *none* **cool:** *40 minutes*

1 pound (4 sticks) unsalted butter, at room temperature

¼ cup oil-packed sun-dried tomatoes, patted dry and roughly chopped

2 tablespoons minced fresh herbs, such as parsley, dill, basil, thyme, or a combination

1 tablespoon minced garlic

Grated zest of 1 lemon

1 teaspoon garlic salt

1 teaspoon freshly cracked black pepper

1. In a large bowl, combine the butter, sun-dried tomatoes, herbs, garlic, lemon zest, garlic salt, and pepper. Refrigerate for 10 minutes.

2. Form the herb butter into 2 logs. Wrap the logs in plastic wrap and refrigerate for 30 minutes or freeze for up to 3 months until needed.

3. To serve from frozen, remove from the freezer and slice off what you need. Use as desired on breads, in soups, and smeared on steak.

Makes about 2 cups

Pretzels

WITH CHEESE DIP

prep: *1 hour 40 minutes*   **cook:** *10 minutes*   **cool:** *none*

I'm the girl who, if given the choice between nachos, a hot dog, and a pretzel, will choose all three and then ask for extra cheese. When we take the family out to a ball game or to a movie, it's safe to assume that I've agreed to go based on the promise of concession stand food. Of course, my kids have inherited some of my eating habits—so when it's time to take my girls to watch their brothers' baseball game, they only ever have one question: Can we get a pretzel with cheese sauce? Creating our own recipe (with cheese sauce, of course) to share here just seemed like the right thing to do.

Two ¼-ounce packets active dry yeast

½ cup plus 1 teaspoon sugar

1¾ cups warm water (95° to 110°F)

5 cups all-purpose flour, plus more for rolling

2 teaspoons kosher salt

1 tablespoon vegetable oil

Cooking spray

⅓ cup baking soda

4 cups boiling water

¼ cup Maldon or other flaky salt

½ cup (1 stick) unsalted butter, melted

Cheese Dip (page 56), for serving

1. In a small bowl, dissolve the yeast and 1 teaspoon of the sugar in the warm water. Set aside until the sugar and yeast are dissolved, about 10 minutes.

2. In a stand mixer fitted with the dough hook, combine the flour, the remaining ½ cup sugar, and the kosher salt. Turn the mixer on low to mix the ingredients. Add the oil and the yeast mixture and mix on medium-low speed for about 5 minutes, until the dough is smooth.

3. Spray a large bowl lightly with cooking spray, place the dough in the bowl, cover with plastic wrap, and let rise in a warm spot until doubled in size, about 1 hour.

4. Meanwhile, preheat the oven to 425°F. Line two baking sheets with parchment paper.

5. Turn the dough onto a lightly floured surface and divide into 16 equal pieces (about 2½ ounces each). Roll each piece into a 24-inch-long rope and twist each rope into a traditional pretzel shape.

6. In a large heatproof bowl, combine the baking soda and boiling water, stirring until the soda is completely dissolved. Dip each pretzel in the soda/water mixture, then place it on one of the prepared pans, leaving 1½ inches between the pretzels. Sprinkle the pretzels with the Maldon salt.

7. Bake until golden brown, about 8 minutes. Brush each pretzel with melted butter and serve immediately with cheese dip.

8. Store in an airtight container at room temperature for up to 2 days.

Makes 12 pretzels

TIP: *To make cinnamon sugar pretzels, leave off the sprinkling of salt, bake the pretzels as directed, brush them with the melted butter, and dip them in a mixture of 1 cup sugar and 3 tablespoons ground cinnamon.*

continued . . .

continued from page 55

Cheese Dip

prep: *10 minutes*   **cook:** *under 10 minutes*   **cool:** *none*

4 tablespoons (½ stick) unsalted butter

¼ cup all-purpose flour

2½ cups milk

6 ounces cream cheese, at room temperature

4 ounces Cheddar cheese, grated (about 1 cup)

2 ounces Gouda cheese, shredded (about ½ cup)

2 teaspoons whole-grain mustard

½ teaspoon smoked paprika

¼ teaspoon cayenne pepper (optional)

½ teaspoon kosher salt

¼ teaspoon freshly ground black pepper

1. In a medium saucepan, melt the butter over medium heat until it bubbles. Add the flour and whisk constantly until well combined. Whisk and cook until thickened, to make a roux, 1 to 2 minutes.

2. Remove from the heat and add the milk. Whisk well. Return to the heat and cook, whisking constantly, until the mixture begins to thicken and will coat the back of a spoon, 4 to 5 minutes.

3. Add the cream cheese, Cheddar, and Gouda and stir until melted. Stir in the mustard, paprika, cayenne (if using), salt, and black pepper and serve immediately.

4. Store in an airtight container in the refrigerator for up to 3 days. Reheat in a small saucepan over medium heat, whisking slowly. Add a teaspoon of milk at a time to thin it out if needed.

Makes 4 cups, to serve 16

Zucchini Bread

prep: *15 minutes*   **cook:** *50 minutes*   **cool:** *30 minutes*

This zucchini bread is all I wanted for breakfast while I was pregnant with Crew. I think the smell of it baking will always take me back to those days filled with anticipation and excitement for our sweet boy to arrive. I made it so often that it became a family favorite, especially for breakfast when I served it freshly baked with eggs and orange juice. Every now and then, I like to bake an extra few batches to share with family and friends.

Cooking spray

1¼ cups vegetable oil

2 cups sugar

4 large eggs

1 tablespoon pure vanilla extract

3 cups all-purpose flour

2 teaspoons ground cinnamon

2 teaspoons baking powder

1 teaspoon baking soda

½ teaspoon kosher salt

3 cups thickly shredded zucchini (about 2 medium)

1 cup crushed walnuts (about 3½ ounces)

1. Preheat the oven to 350°F. Spray a 9 × 9-inch baking pan lightly with cooking spray.

2. In a large bowl, whisk together the vegetable oil, sugar, eggs, and vanilla until smooth.

3. In a medium bowl, whisk together the flour, cinnamon, baking powder, baking soda, and salt. Add the flour mixture to the egg/sugar mixture and mix until just combined.

4. Wrap the zucchini in a clean kitchen towel and squeeze out any excess liquid. Fold the zucchini and walnuts into the batter.

5. Pour the batter into the prepared pan and spread it evenly. Bake until a tester inserted in the center comes out clean, about 50 minutes. Cool on a wire rack until completely cool, about 30 minutes.

6. Store in an airtight container at room temperature for up to 3 days.

Makes about 9 servings

TIP: *Eat warm with a pat of butter.*

Prize Pig

prep: *50 minutes, plus 1 hour 30 minutes chilling*   **cook:** *15 minutes*   **cool:** *none*

1 pound peppered bacon

4 cups self-rising flour, plus more for the work surface

2 tablespoons baking powder

1 teaspoon baking soda

¾ pound (3 sticks) cold salted butter, cut into ½-inch cubes

2 large eggs, whisked, plus 1 large egg for brushing

1½ to 2 cups buttermilk, or as needed, plus 1 tablespoon buttermilk for brushing

4 ounces Cheddar cheese, grated (about 1 cup)

4 ounces white Cheddar cheese, grated (about 1 cup)

¼ cup minced chives

1. Line a sheet pan with parchment paper and lay the bacon strips on the pan. Position a rack in the top third of the oven, place the sheet pan on the rack, and preheat the oven to 400°F. Let the bacon cook as the oven preheats until crispy, about 20 minutes. Turn off the oven and transfer the bacon to paper towels to absorb the excess grease. When cool enough to handle, dice the bacon and set aside.

2. In a large bowl, whisk together the flour, baking powder, and baking soda. Add the butter and use a pastry blender or your fingers to cut the butter into the flour until the pieces are even and about the size of peas.

3. Use a wooden spoon to stir in 2 eggs until combined. Stir in 1½ cups of the buttermilk until the dough comes together into a really sticky mass. If it is not very sticky, add more buttermilk, 1 tablespoon at a time, mixing well after each addition. Add the diced bacon, cheeses, and chives and use your hands to mix into the biscuit dough until well incorporated, but do not overmix. Cover the bowl and refrigerate for at least 1 hour and up to overnight.

4. Scrape the dough onto a lightly floured work surface. Use your hands to press it into a large round roughly 14 inches across.

5. Line a baking sheet with parchment paper. Use a 3½-inch biscuit cutter to cut out about 20 rounds. Transfer the biscuits to the lined pan, arranging them so that they all are touching. (If making ahead, arrange the biscuits on a baking sheet, not touching, and freeze until solid, then transfer to a zip-top bag and freeze for up to 2 weeks. There is no need to thaw before baking.)

6. In a small dish, whisk the remaining 1 egg and 1 tablespoon buttermilk. Brush the mixture over the biscuits. Refrigerate for 30 minutes.

7. Meanwhile, preheat the oven to 400°F.

8. Transfer the biscuits to the oven and bake until golden brown, about 15 minutes. Let cool slightly in the pan on a rack.

9. Store in a zip-top bag or airtight container at room temperature for up to 2 days.

Makes about 20 biscuits

TIP: *The biscuits are best the day they are made (and ideally fresh from the oven!).*

Cinnamon Swirl Bread

prep: *2 hours 30 minutes*   **cook:** *35 minutes*   **cool:** *40 minutes*

After years of baking at home and now developing recipes for the bakery, I've learned something about myself: I'll pretty much take cinnamon in any form, especially when it's swirled inside a warm, buttery bread. What I love about this recipe is that it yields a bread that isn't so sweet that it can't be enjoyed for breakfast but is still sweet enough to curb any after-dinner cravings. Making bread can seem like an intimidating task, but the hands-on work for this recipe is only about 30 minutes. That's what I call a win-win.

bread

¼ cup warm water (95° to 110°F)

One ¼-ounce packet active dry yeast

½ cup plus 1 teaspoon sugar

3¾ cups bread flour, plus more for rolling

1 teaspoon kosher salt

4 tablespoons (½ stick) unsalted butter, at room temperature

1 cup warm whole milk (100°F)

Cooking spray

filling

1 tablespoon ground cinnamon

⅔ cup sugar

egg wash

1 large egg

2 tablespoons whole milk

1. To make the bread: In a small bowl, combine the warm water, yeast, and 1 teaspoon of the sugar. Let stand until foamy, about 5 minutes.

2. In a stand mixer fitted with the dough hook, combine the flour, remaining ½ cup sugar, and the salt. With the mixer on low speed, slowly add the yeast mixture, butter, and milk. Allow to mix for about 1 minute, then turn the speed to medium-high and mix until the dough forms into a ball, about 5 minutes.

3. Spray a medium bowl with vegetable oil and place the dough in the bowl. Cover with plastic wrap and set in a warm place until the dough has doubled in size, about 1 hour.

4. Meanwhile, to make the filling: In a small bowl, stir together the cinnamon and sugar until combined.

5. Spray two 8 × 4-inch loaf pans with cooking spray and set aside.

6. Punch down the dough to release the air, then divide it in half. On a lightly floured surface, roll one piece of dough out into an 8 × 16-inch rectangle.

7. To make the egg wash: In a small bowl, whisk together the egg and milk. Using a pastry brush, brush the egg wash all over the surface of the rolled-out dough. Sprinkle with half of the filling.

8. Starting with a shorter side, tightly roll the dough away from yourself. Place the loaf seam side down in one of the prepared pans. Repeat with the second dough ball, some more egg wash (reserve and refrigerate the remaining egg wash), and the remaining filling. Place seam side down in the other prepared pan.

9. Lightly cover each pan with plastic wrap and set in a warm area to rise for about 1 hour.

continued . . .

continued from page 61

10. While the dough is rising, preheat the oven to 375°F.

11. Gently remove the plastic wrap from the dough and brush the tops with the reserved egg wash. Bake until the bread is a dark golden color, about 35 minutes. You can also test for doneness by turning it onto the counter and thumping it (it is done if it sounds hollow) or by inserting a thermometer into the loaf—it should read between 190° and 200°F.

12. Let the bread cool in the pans for 10 minutes, then transfer to a wire rack to cool at least 30 minutes more before slicing.

13. Store in a zip-top bag or airtight container at room temperature for up to 3 days.

Makes 2 loaves

Pumpkin Cream Cheese Bread

prep: *15 minutes*   **cook:** *1 hour 10 minutes*   **cool:** *1 hour 20 minutes*

Cooking spray

cream cheese filling

4 ounces cream cheese, at room temperature

3 tablespoons sugar

1 egg yolk

½ teaspoon pure vanilla extract

bread

1¾ cups all-purpose flour

1½ cups sugar

1 teaspoon baking soda

1 teaspoon ground cinnamon

½ teaspoon kosher salt

¼ teaspoon ground nutmeg

1 cup canned unsweetened pumpkin puree (not pie filling)

8 tablespoons (1 stick) unsalted butter, melted

1 large egg

⅓ cup whole milk

1 teaspoon pure vanilla extract

1. Preheat the oven to 350°F. Spray a 9 × 5-inch loaf pan with cooking spray.

2. To make the cream cheese filling: In a stand mixer fitted with the paddle attachment, beat the cream cheese, sugar, egg yolk, and vanilla on medium speed. Transfer to a medium bowl and set aside.

3. To make the bread: In a medium bowl, whisk together the flour, sugar, baking soda, cinnamon, salt, and nutmeg until combined.

4. In a stand mixer fitted with the paddle attachment, combine the pumpkin puree, melted butter, egg, milk, and vanilla and stir on low speed until the mixture is smooth.

5. With the mixer still on low, gradually add the flour mixture until just combined. Increase the speed to medium-high for about 30 seconds to mix thoroughly.

6. Pour one-third of the pumpkin batter into the prepared pan. Top with half of the cream cheese filling and spread it out evenly with a spatula, then pour one-third of the pumpkin batter over the filling. Spread the remaining filling on top, then dollop the remaining pumpkin batter on top. With a knife, cut through the batter several times to create a swirl effect.

7. Bake until a tester inserted in the bread comes out clean, about 1 hour 10 minutes. Let cool in the pan for about 20 minutes, then remove the bread to a rack to cool completely, about 1 hour.

8. Store in an airtight container in the refrigerator for up to 3 days.

Makes 1 loaf

Blueberry Muffins

WITH STREUSEL TOPPING

prep: *20 minutes*   **cook:** *under 30 minutes*   **cool:** *none*

streusel

¼ cup plus 1 tablespoon sugar

2 tablespoons all-purpose
  flour

2 tablespoons cold unsalted
  butter

muffins

Cooking spray

1⅓ cups all-purpose flour

1 teaspoon baking powder

½ teaspoon kosher salt

8 tablespoons (1 stick)
  unsalted butter, softened

1 cup sugar

2 large eggs

1 teaspoon pure vanilla extract

½ cup sour cream

1 cup frozen blueberries,
  unthawed

1. To make the streusel: In a medium bowl, stir together the sugar and flour. Use a pastry blender or your fingers to cut in the butter, mixing it thoroughly until it resembles coarse crumbs. Refrigerate until ready to use.

2. To make the muffins: Preheat the oven to 350°F. Spray 12 cups of a muffin tin lightly with cooking spray or line them with cupcake liners.

3. In a medium bowl, stir together the flour, baking powder, and salt.

4. In a stand mixer fitted with the paddle attachment, cream the butter and sugar on medium speed until light and fluffy, about 2 minutes. Reduce the speed to low and slowly add the eggs and vanilla. Turn the mixer to medium-high speed and mix until well incorporated.

5. With the mixer on low speed, add half of the flour mixture, then half of the sour cream. Add the remaining flour and sour cream and mix until well incorporated. Fold in the blueberries.

6. Using a ¼-cup measure, fill the prepared muffin cups three-quarters full. Sprinkle streusel on top of each muffin.

7. Bake until a tester inserted into the center of a muffin comes out clean, 24 to 28 minutes. Serve warm.

8. Store in an airtight container at room temperature for up to 2 days.

Makes 12 muffins

Monkey Bread

prep: *2 hours 40 minutes*　　**cook:** *under 35 minutes*　　**cool:** *5 minutes*

This is one of my kids' favorite snacks to come home to after school. Fortunately for me, they share my opinion that few combinations are better than doughy bread, butter, and cinnamon sugar!

dough

One ¼-ounce packet active dry yeast

¼ cup plus 1 teaspoon granulated sugar

⅓ cup warm water (95° to 110°F)

1 cup whole milk, warmed slightly

2 tablespoons unsalted butter, melted

3¾ cups all-purpose flour, plus more for the work surface

2 teaspoons kosher salt

Cooking spray

caramel sauce

8 tablespoons (1 stick) unsalted butter

1 cup packed light brown sugar

1 teaspoon pure vanilla extract

assembly

1 cup granulated sugar

2 tablespoons ground cinnamon

Nonstick baking spray

1. To make the dough: In a small bowl, dissolve the yeast 1 teaspoon of the granulated sugar in the warm water and let sit for about 5 minutes.

2. In a separate small bowl, whisk the milk, butter, and remaining ¼ cup sugar.

3. In a stand mixer fitted with the dough hook, combine the flour and salt. With the mixer on low, slowly pour the yeast and milk/butter mixtures in. After the dough comes together, increase the speed to medium and mix for 6 or 7 minutes. The dough should still be on the sticky side but not overly wet.

4. Spray a large bowl lightly with cooking spray and set the dough in the bowl to proof. Cover the bowl with a damp towel or plastic wrap and let the dough rise in a warm place until it has doubled in size, 1 hour to 1 hour 30 minutes.

5. Lightly flour a work surface. Form the dough into a round about 1 inch thick and use a pizza cutter to cut the dough into 1-inch-wide pieces. Set aside.

6. To make the caramel sauce: In a small saucepan, combine the butter and brown sugar and cook over medium heat, stirring often, until the sugar is dissolved, about 2 minutes. Add the vanilla and stir to incorporate. Set aside.

7. In a gallon zip-top bag, combine the granulated sugar and cinnamon and shake to mix. Place 3 to 5 of the dough pieces in the cinnamon sugar and gently shake to coat each evenly. Remove to a tray. Repeat until all the dough is covered in cinnamon sugar. Discard any extra cinnamon sugar.

8. Spray a large (16-cup) Bundt pan with nonstick baking spray and drizzle half of the caramel sauce around the bottom of the pan. Arrange the dough pieces evenly in the pan. Drizzle with the remaining sauce. Cover with plastic wrap and let rise until doubled in size, about 45 minutes.

9. Meanwhile, preheat the oven to 350°F.

10. Uncover the pan and bake until puffy and crispy on top, 28 to 33 minutes. Let cool for 5 minutes. Place a plate on the pan and invert it to remove the bread.

11. Store in an airtight container for up to 2 days.

Makes 8 servings

Coffee Cake

prep: *20 minutes*   **cook:** *under 35 minutes*   **cool:** *none*

streusel

¾ cup sugar

½ cup all-purpose flour

2 teaspoons ground cinnamon

5 tablespoons cold unsalted
  butter, cubed

cake

Cooking spray

2 cups all-purpose flour

2 teaspoons baking powder

½ teaspoon kosher salt

8 tablespoons (1 stick)
  unsalted butter, at room
  temperature

¾ cup sugar

1 large egg

¾ cup whole milk

2 teaspoons pure vanilla
  extract

1. To make the streusel: In a medium bowl, combine the sugar, flour, and cinnamon. Cut in the butter with a pastry blender or your fingers until the mixture resembles coarse crumbs. Refrigerate until ready to use.

2. To make the cake: Preheat the oven to 350°F. Spray a 9 × 9-inch baking pan lightly with cooking spray.

3. In a medium bowl, stir together the flour, baking powder, and salt.

4. In a stand mixer fitted with the paddle attachment, cream the butter and sugar until light and fluffy, about 4 minutes. Scrape the sides down. Add the egg, milk, and vanilla and mix on low speed until the ingredients start coming together. With the machine running, add the flour mixture, mixing until fully incorporated.

5. Spread the batter in the prepared baking pan and sprinkle the streusel over the batter.

6. Bake until a tester inserted in the center comes out clean, 30 to 35 minutes. Serve warm.

7. Store in an airtight container at room temperature for up to 2 days.

Makes 12 servings

Maple Walnut Scones

prep: *20 minutes, plus 15 minutes chilling*   **cook:** *under 20 minutes*   **cool:** *40 minutes*

scones

½ cup chopped walnuts
(2 ounces)

1¾ cups all-purpose flour, plus
more for the work surface

½ cup granulated sugar

1 tablespoon baking powder

½ teaspoon kosher salt

6 tablespoons (¾ stick) cold
unsalted butter, cut into
½-inch cubes

1 large egg

⅓ cup heavy cream

1 teaspoon pure maple extract

1 teaspoon pure vanilla extract

glaze

½ cup powdered sugar

2 tablespoons heavy cream

¼ teaspoon pure maple
extract

1. Preheat the oven to 375°F. Line a baking sheet with parchment paper.

2. To make the scones: Spread the walnuts on the lined pan and toast in the oven until lightly browned, 8 to 10 minutes. Set aside to cool, about 10 minutes. Keep the pan lined with parchment for baking the scones.

3. Meanwhile, in a large bowl, whisk together the flour, sugar, baking powder, and salt. Add the butter cubes and toss to coat. Using a pastry blender or your fingers, cut in the butter until it resembles coarse crumbs. Add the toasted walnuts and stir to combine.

4. In a medium bowl, whisk together the egg, cream, maple extract, and vanilla extract. Stir the wet ingredients into the flour mixture and mix until a dough is formed.

5. Lightly flour a work surface. Pat the dough into a round about 8 inches in diameter and ½ inch thick and cut it into 8 wedges, as you would a pizza. Carefully place each scone on the baking sheet, keeping about 2 inches between the scones. Refrigerate, uncovered, for 15 minutes.

6. Transfer to the oven and bake until the bottoms of the scones are lightly browned, 15 to 20 minutes. Let the scones cool for 5 to 10 minutes, then transfer them to a rack to finish cooling, about 30 minutes.

7. Meanwhile, to make the glaze: In a medium bowl, whisk together the powdered sugar, cream, and maple extract until smooth.

8. Drizzle the glaze on the cooled scones.

9. Store in an airtight container at room temperature for up to 2 days.

Makes 8 scones

Blueberry Sweet Rolls

WITH LEMON GLAZE

SERVED AT
magnolia press
WACO · TX

prep: *2 hours 15 minutes, plus 30 minutes chilling*   **cook:** *under 20 minutes*   **cool:** *5 minutes*

This is the first recipe we developed for our coffee shop, Magnolia Press. After a few rounds, I knew we were onto something good—a classic gooey cinnamon roll elevated by the sweetness of blueberries and balanced with the tartness of lemon glaze.

sweet rolls

1 cup warm whole milk (95°
   to 110°F)

One ¼-ounce packet active
   dry yeast

2 tablespoons granulated
   sugar

3 tablespoons unsalted butter,
   at room temperature

1 large egg

3 cups all-purpose flour, plus
   more for rolling

1 teaspoon kosher salt

Baking spray

filling

1 cup frozen blueberries

⅓ cup granulated sugar

1 tablespoon cornstarch

lemon glaze

Grated zest of 1 lemon

3 tablespoons fresh lemon
   juice

1 tablespoon unsalted butter,
   melted

1¾ cups powdered sugar

Pinch of kosher salt

1. In a stand mixer fitted with the dough hook, combine the warm milk, yeast, granulated sugar, butter, and egg. Gradually mix in the flour and salt on low speed until incorporated, about 5 minutes. Increase the speed to medium and beat until the dough is smooth, elastic, and slightly sticky, about 3 minutes.

2. Transfer the dough to a lightly sprayed medium stainless steel bowl. Cover with plastic wrap and let rise in a warm area until doubled in size, about 1 hour.

3. Meanwhile, in a small saucepan, combine the blueberries, granulated sugar, and cornstarch. Cook over medium-high heat, stirring often, as the berries break down and release their liquid. Bring to a boil, stirring constantly, until the liquid thickens and is syrupy, 3 to 4 minutes. Transfer to a bowl and chill, uncovered, until completely cool, about 30 minutes.

4. Lightly spray a 9 × 13-inch baking pan with baking spray.

5. Punch down the dough to release the air and transfer to a lightly floured surface. Roll the dough into a 12 × 18-inch rectangle, dusting with up to ¼ cup flour as needed to prevent sticking.

6. Using a spatula, spread the filling over the dough, leaving a ½-inch border. Starting on a short side, roll up the dough tightly away from you to make a 12-inch-long roll. Using a sharp knife or uncoated dental floss, cut the dough into twelve 1-inch-thick slices. Place them cut side up in the prepared pan, cover with plastic wrap, and let rise until doubled in size, about 45 minutes.

7. Preheat the oven to 350°F.

8. Bake the rolls until lightly browned, 16 to 18 minutes.

9. Meanwhile, to make the lemon glaze: In a small bowl, whisk together the lemon zest, lemon juice, melted butter, powdered sugar, and salt.

10. Let the rolls cool for 5 minutes. Drizzle the glaze on top and serve.

11. Store in an airtight container at room temperature for 1 to 2 days.

Makes 12 rolls

CHAPTER THREE

Breakfast & Brunch

BREAKFAST PLAYS A PART IN SETTING

THE PACE AND RHYTHM OF OUR DAYS—

WHETHER IT'S A GRAB AND GO OR TAKE IT

SLOW KIND OF MORNING, THIS IS WHERE

WE FUEL UP FOR ALL THAT'S IN STORE

Mushroom Gruyère Quiche

prep: *30 minutes*　　**cook:** *under 30 minutes*　　**cool:** *15 minutes*

4 large eggs

1½ cups half-and-half

2 tablespoons chopped chives

2 teaspoons grated lemon zest

2 tablespoons olive oil

1 pound assorted fresh
　mushrooms (button,
　shiitake, oyster,
　chanterelle), sliced

2 teaspoons fresh thyme
　leaves

½ teaspoon kosher salt

½ teaspoon freshly ground
　black pepper

2 tablespoons unsalted butter

6 ounces Gruyère cheese,
　grated (about 1½ cups)

1 unbaked Tart Shell
　(page 27)

1. Preheat the oven to 375°F.

2. In a large bowl, whisk together the eggs, half-and-half, chives, and lemon zest.

3. In a large skillet, heat the olive oil over medium-high heat. Add the mushrooms and sauté until browned to a slight crisp, about 5 minutes. Sprinkle the mushrooms with the thyme, salt, and pepper and stir well. Add the butter and sauté until the mushrooms are tender, about 4 minutes. Remove and let cool slightly, about 10 minutes.

4. Spread ½ cup of the Gruyère on the bottom of the tart shell. Pour half of the egg mixture over the Gruyère and top with half of the mushroom mixture. Repeat with another ½ cup Gruyère and the rest of the egg and mushroom mixtures. Top evenly with the remaining ½ cup Gruyère.

5. Transfer to the oven and bake until the edges of the tart shell are golden brown, 25 to 30 minutes. If you want a browned surface on the quiche, broil for the last 5 minutes, watching carefully so that the quiche doesn't burn. Place a strip of foil around the tart shell edges if they are getting too brown.

6. Let the quiche cool slightly, about 15 minutes. Slice and serve warm or at room temperature.

7. Store in an airtight container in the refrigerator for up to 2 days. Reheat in a 350°F oven (the microwave is not recommended).

Makes 6 to 8 servings

Rancher's Steak & Eggs

prep: *15 minutes*   **cook:** *30 minutes*   **cool:** *none*

Chip's granddad was a quintessential Texas rancher. I never had the chance to meet JB, but I feel like I know him through Chip's stories, and I like to imagine that this is the kind of meal he'd choose to start his day with. I've been told that Chip is like his granddad in a lot of ways: both like working with their hands, both are industrious, and both share a deep love and appreciation for a good, hearty breakfast.

One 1-pound rib eye steak

1 teaspoon kosher salt

1 tablespoon Worcestershire

4 tablespoons (½ stick) butter

1 small garlic clove, minced

2 tablespoons olive oil

One 20-ounce bag hash
    browns, thawed and
    patted dry

4 large eggs

1 tablespoon minced chives

1 teaspoon freshly ground
    black pepper

1. Preheat the oven to 350°F.

2. Rub the steak with ½ teaspoon of the salt and ½ tablespoon of the Worcestershire. In a large cast-iron skillet, melt 2 tablespoons of the butter over high heat. Add the steak to the pan and sear for 5 to 6 minutes. Flip the steak and sear for another 5 to 6 minutes for medium (the internal temp will be 140°F). Add the garlic in the last minute of cooking, stirring until just cooked through. Don't let it burn.

3. Transfer the steak to a cutting board to rest and spoon the garlic over the steak.

4. Meanwhile, wipe the skillet clean. Set it over medium-high heat and add the olive oil and the remaining 2 tablespoons butter. Spread the hash browns in the skillet in an even layer and cook without disturbing until browned and crispy, 8 to 10 minutes. Flip the hash browns, give them a stir, and spread them again into an even layer.

5. Crack the eggs over the hash browns. Transfer the skillet to the oven and bake until the egg whites are cooked and the yolks are at the desired doneness, about 8 minutes.

6. Slice the steak against the grain and at an angle to the cutting board. Serve alongside the hash browns and eggs. Sprinkle with the chives, pepper, and the remaining ½ teaspoon of salt and ½ tablespoon of Worcestershire.

Makes 4 servings

Bacon & Leek Quiche

prep: *20 minutes*   **cook:** *1 hour 5 minutes*   **cool:** *15 minutes*

1 pound bacon

5 large eggs

1 cup heavy cream

3 large leeks (white and light-green parts only), thinly sliced

¼ teaspoon kosher salt

½ teaspoon ground white pepper

8 ounces Gruyère cheese, shredded (about 2 cups)

1 unbaked 9-inch pie shell, store-bought or homemade (see page 23)

1. Preheat the oven to 350°F.

2. Arrange the bacon on a sheet pan. Bake until crispy, about 30 minutes. Line a second baking sheet with paper towels and transfer the bacon to the paper towels to drain. Roughly chop the bacon into ½-inch pieces and set aside.

3. In a large bowl, whisk together the eggs and cream until combined and smooth. Stir in the bacon, leeks, salt, white pepper, and Gruyère. Pour the mixture into the pie shell.

4. Transfer to the oven and bake until a toothpick inserted into the center comes out clean, about 35 minutes.

5. Remove from the oven and transfer to a wire rack to cool for 15 minutes to allow the eggs to set.

6. Slice and serve warm or at room temperature.

7. Store in an airtight container in the refrigerator for up to 4 days.

Makes 8 servings

Pecan Pancakes
WITH MAPLE BUTTER

prep: *under 15 minutes*   **cook:** *under 20 minutes*   **cool:** *none*

1 cup pecans

2 cups all-purpose flour

¼ cup granulated sugar

1½ teaspoons baking powder

1½ teaspoons baking soda

1 teaspoon kosher salt

2½ cups buttermilk

2 large eggs, separated

1 teaspoon pure vanilla extract

2 tablespoons unsalted butter, melted

Maple Butter (page 91), for serving

Pure maple syrup, for serving

1. Preheat the oven to 250°F. Set a wire rack on a sheet pan.

2. In a large dry skillet, toast the pecans over medium-high heat, stirring constantly, until fragrant, 3 to 5 minutes. Remove from the pan and let cool completely. Coarsely chop and set aside.

3. In a large bowl, whisk together the flour, sugar, baking powder, baking soda, and salt. Make a well in the center. Pour the buttermilk and egg yolks into the well and whisk by hand until just incorporated (there will be lumps). Add the vanilla and melted butter and stir gently until incorporated. Do not overwhisk. (The batter can be refrigerated for up to 1 hour.)

4. Just before cooking the pancakes, in a large bowl, with an electric mixer, beat the egg whites until soft peaks form, about 1 minute. Fold gently into the batter.

5. Heat a large nonstick griddle to 300°F or a nonstick skillet over medium-low heat for about 5 minutes.

6. Working in batches to avoid overcrowding, use a measuring cup to ladle ⅓ cup batter onto the griddle or skillet for each pancake. Cook until the pancakes begin to bubble in the middle and the bottom edges brown, 2 to 4 minutes. Flip the pancakes and cook until the other side is slightly browned, 1 to 2 minutes more. Transfer each batch of pancakes to the wire rack and place them in the oven to keep warm until ready to serve.

7. Stack the pancakes, top with pats of maple butter, and sprinkle with the toasted pecans. Pour your favorite maple syrup over the top and serve.

8. Store in an airtight container in the refrigerator overnight.

Makes 12 pancakes

French Toast

WITH VANILLA MAPLE SYRUP

prep: *15 minutes*   **cook:** *30 minutes*   **cool:** *none*

There is a time and place for the finer things in life—the things that are clearly and without question made to be extraordinary. It's fun to indulge in those things from time to time; however, what I find myself drawn to more regularly is the unexpected delight that comes from taking something ordinary and making it special. French toast is one of those unexpectedly simple dishes that always feels intentional. No one is ever disappointed to hear we're having French toast for breakfast (or dinner!), especially when paired with Chip's favorite—strawberry butter.

12 tablespoons (1½ sticks) unsalted butter

2 tablespoons light brown sugar

½ teaspoon ground cinnamon

⅓ cup heavy cream

1 teaspoon pure vanilla extract

4 large eggs

12 slices (¾ inch thick) white bread, brioche, or challah

⅓ cup Vanilla Maple Syrup (page 90) or pure maple syrup, warmed

6 tablespoons Strawberry Butter (page 90)

Powdered sugar, for dusting

1. Preheat the oven to 250°F. Set a wire rack on a sheet pan.

2. In a large skillet, heat 6 tablespoons of the butter over low heat until just melted.

3. Meanwhile, in a large bowl, stir together the brown sugar and cinnamon. Pour the melted butter over the cinnamon/sugar mixture in the bowl and whisk quickly to incorporate. (Reserve the skillet.) Whisk the cream and vanilla into the butter/brown sugar mixture until well combined, about 30 seconds. Add the eggs and whisk until completely smooth, 1 to 2 minutes. Set aside.

4. Heat the skillet over medium heat. Add 1 tablespoon of the butter to the pan and swirl to coat; it should start to bubble.

5. Working with 2 or 3 slices of bread at a time, depending on how many will fit into the skillet without crowding, dip the bread slices into the bowl (or pour the mixture into a shallow dish), making sure to coat both sides well. Let the excess mixture drip off into the bowl.

6. Place the coated slices in the pan and cook until slightly browned on both sides, 5 to 6 minutes total, flipping halfway through. As each batch is cooked, transfer to the wire rack on the sheet pan and set the sheet pan in the oven to keep warm until ready to serve.

7. Repeat to cook the rest of the French toast, using the remaining butter to coat the pan between batches.

8. Drizzle the French toast evenly with warmed syrup and top each plate with 1 tablespoon strawberry butter. Dust with powdered sugar and serve.

Makes 6 servings

Waffles

WITH STRAWBERRY BUTTER

prep: *15 minutes* **cook:** *under 45 minutes* **cool:** *none*

Cooking spray

2 cups all-purpose flour

2 teaspoons baking powder

¾ teaspoon kosher salt

⅓ cup sugar

2 large eggs, separated

2 cups milk

½ cup vegetable oil

1 teaspoon pure vanilla extract

Strawberry Butter
(page 90), for serving

Vanilla Maple Syrup,
(page 90), for serving

1. Spray a waffle iron with cooking spray and preheat it to medium-high.

2. Sift the flour, baking powder, salt, and sugar into a medium bowl.

3. In a large bowl, with an electric mixer, beat the egg whites until stiff peaks form, about 2 minutes.

4. In another large bowl, stir together the egg yolks, milk, oil, and vanilla. Add the flour mixture and mix just until fully incorporated. Gently fold in the beaten egg whites.

5. For each waffle, spoon ½ cup batter onto the waffle iron and cook until the waffle is golden and releases easily, 5 to 7 minutes. Serve hot with strawberry butter and syrup.

Makes 6 servings

Strawberry Butter

SERVED AT
magnolia table
WACO · TX

prep: *10 minutes*   **cook:** *none*   **cool:** *none*

1 cup (2 sticks) unsalted
   butter, at room
   temperature

¼ cup strawberry preserves,
   homemade or store-bought

⅛ teaspoon sea salt

1. In a stand mixer fitted with the whisk, beat the butter on high speed until light and fluffy, 4 to 5 minutes. Turn the speed to low and add the preserves 1 tablespoon at a time until well incorporated. Sprinkle in the salt and beat on high until light and fluffy, 1 to 2 minutes.

2. Transfer to an airtight container. Store in the refrigerator for up to 5 days or in the freezer for up to 1 month. Serve at room temperature.

Makes about 1 cup (sixteen 1-tablespoon servings)

Vanilla Maple Syrup

prep: *5 minutes*   **cook:** *20 minutes*   **cool:** *none*

1 cup granulated sugar

2 teaspoons pure vanilla
   extract

2 teaspoons pure maple
   extract

1. In a medium saucepan, combine the sugar and 1 cup water and bring to a boil. Add the extracts, reduce the heat to the lowest setting, and simmer, stirring occasionally, for 20 minutes.

2. Store in a mason jar in the refrigerator for up to 2 weeks. Reheat in a saucepan over the lowest heat setting before serving.

Makes about 1½ cups

Maple Butter

prep: *10 minutes, plus 20 minutes chilling*   **cook:** *none*   **cool:** *none*

1 cup (2 sticks) unsalted
  butter, at room
  temperature

⅓ cup plus 2 tablespoons pure
  maple syrup

½ teaspoon kosher salt

1. In a stand mixer fitted with the whisk, beat the butter on high speed until light and fluffy, 4 to 5 minutes. Turn the speed to low and slowly pour in the syrup. Mix until well incorporated. Add the salt, turn the speed to high, and beat for 2 minutes, stopping to scrape down the bowl halfway through.

2. Scrape the butter onto parchment paper and roll into a log. Twist the ends of the parchment paper to secure and refrigerate for 20 minutes.

3. Unwrap the log and slice the butter into pats when ready to serve.

4. Store in an airtight container in the refrigerator for up to 7 days or in the freezer for up to 1 month.

Makes about 1 cup (sixteen 1-tablespoon servings)

Huevos Rancheros

prep: *15 minutes*　　**cook:** *1 hour*　　**cool:** *none*

It doesn't matter what type of restaurant we're dining in or what time of day it is, if huevos rancheros is on the menu, there's a good chance the Gaines boys are going to order it. Our take is served on a fried corn tortilla, full of fresh add-ins, and it always hits the mark for my boys.

5 tablespoons unsalted butter

2½ cups chopped tomatoes (about 2 medium)

1 cup thinly sliced yellow onion (about 1 small)

1 tablespoon chopped seeded jalapeño, plus thin slices for garnish

1 garlic clove, minced

1¼ teaspoons kosher salt, plus more to taste

½ teaspoon ground cumin

6 tablespoons olive oil

6 corn tortillas, store-bought or homemade (see page 31)

One 15.5-ounce can black beans, rinsed well and drained

6 large eggs

Coarsely ground black pepper

2 tablespoons fresh cilantro leaves

2 tablespoons chopped green onions

2 ounces Cotija cheese, crumbled (about ½ cup)

Lime wedges, for serving (optional)

1. In a large saucepan, heat 1 tablespoon of the butter over medium heat until sizzling. Add the tomatoes, onion, jalapeño, garlic, and 1 teaspoon of the salt. Cook, stirring occasionally, until the vegetables are very tender, 20 to 25 minutes. Add ¼ cup water and the cumin. Using an immersion blender, process until the sauce has the consistency of a chunky tomato sauce, 20 to 30 seconds. Set the ranchero sauce aside. (If making ahead, the ranchero sauce will keep for 3 to 5 days in an airtight container in the refrigerator.)

2. Line a baking sheet with paper towels. In a large skillet, heat 1 tablespoon of the oil over medium heat until shimmering. Add 1 of the tortillas and cook until slightly puffed and golden brown, turning once, 2 to 3 minutes. Transfer to the lined baking sheet. Repeat with the remaining 5 tablespoons of oil and 5 corn tortillas.

3. In a small saucepan, combine the black beans, ¼ cup water, and the remaining ¼ teaspoon salt. Cook over medium heat, stirring often, until hot, about 5 minutes. Cover and keep warm.

4. In a large nonstick skillet, melt 2 tablespoons of the butter over medium heat. Crack 3 eggs into the pan and cook, undisturbed, until the whites begin to set, about 30 seconds. Add 1 tablespoon water, cover the skillet, and cook until the whites are set, about 1 minute. Transfer the eggs to a plate. Repeat with the remaining 3 eggs and 2 tablespoons butter. Sprinkle with salt and pepper to taste.

5. Spoon about ¼ cup black beans and ⅓ cup ranchero sauce on top of each tortilla and top with an egg. Sprinkle the cilantro, green onions, Cotija, and jalapeño slices over each serving and squeeze with lime wedges (if using).

Makes 6 servings

Migas Casserole

prep: *40 minutes*   **cook:** *50 minutes*   **cool:** *none*

1 tablespoon unsalted butter, plus more for the baking dish

1 tablespoon canola oil (optional; if using tortillas)

Four 6-inch corn tortillas, store-bought or homemade (see page 31), or 2 cups of your favorite tortilla chips

1 tablespoon olive oil

1 large green bell pepper, cut into ¼-inch dice

1 large red bell pepper, cut into ¼-inch dice

½ medium yellow onion, cut into ¼-inch dice

1 large jalapeño, seeded and finely minced

4 medium tomatoes, seeded and chopped

One 15-ounce can black beans, rinsed well and drained

2 teaspoons ground cumin

2½ teaspoons kosher salt

1 teaspoon freshly ground black pepper

12 large eggs

¾ cup half-and-half

12 ounces Cheddar cheese (about 3 cups), grated

⅓ cup chopped fresh cilantro

1 large avocado, pitted, peeled, and diced, for serving (optional)

1. Preheat the oven to 375°F. Butter a 9 × 13-inch baking dish.

2. If you're using tortillas, in a large skillet, bring the canola oil to a sizzle over high heat. Using tongs, add the tortillas, one at a time, frying until crispy, 15 to 20 seconds per side. Remove and set on paper towels to drain the excess oil. Set aside to cool and crisp up, 1 to 2 minutes. Crumble the fried tortillas or tortilla chips.

3. Return the skillet to medium-high heat and add the 1 tablespoon butter and the olive oil. As soon as the butter begins to melt, add the bell peppers and onion, and cook, stirring occasionally, until fragrant and beginning to brown, 6 to 8 minutes.

4. Add the jalapeño and tomatoes and cook until the tomatoes have reduced and the sauce has thickened, about 4 minutes. Add the black beans, sprinkle with the cumin, salt, and pepper, and give a good stir to mix everything evenly. Remove the skillet from the heat and set aside to cool for 10 minutes.

5. Meanwhile, in a large bowl, whisk the eggs and half-and-half until well combined, 1 to 2 minutes.

6. In the prepared baking dish, combine the veggie mixture, egg mixture, 2 cups of the Cheddar, the crumbled tortillas or chips, and half the cilantro. Stir until well combined.

7. Cover tightly with foil and bake for 35 minutes. Remove the foil and sprinkle with the remaining 1 cup Cheddar. Bake, uncovered, until set in the middle and nicely browned, 10 to 15 minutes more.

8. Serve hot, topped with diced avocado (if using) and the remaining cilantro.

9. Store in a covered container in the refrigerator for up to 2 days.

Makes 8 to 10

TIP: *If desired, garnish with sliced green onions, quartered small limes, and Pickled Red Onion (see page 165).*

Farmhouse Omelet

prep: *40 minutes*   **cook:** *25 minutes*   **cool:** *none*

Our family loves this omelet because there's something in it for everyone, plus it can be easily modified for any day of the week. While the basics stay the same—beaten eggs fried in a pan—we'll change up the ingredients we toss in based on what's growing in the garden or whatever we already have on hand. Other times it's the essentials we crave most: eggs, cheese, and flaky salt. This specific recipe has been our go-to lately—and on many mornings, it's an all-hands-on-deck kind of meal.

4 slices thick-cut bacon, diced

6 tablespoons (¾ stick) unsalted butter

1 cup washed, small-diced new potatoes

½ small yellow onion, finely diced

8 large eggs, at room temperature

¼ cup heavy cream, at room temperature

¼ teaspoon smoked paprika

½ teaspoon kosher salt

½ teaspoon freshly ground black pepper

8 cherry tomatoes, quartered

2 tablespoons minced chives, plus more for garnish

1 tablespoon chopped fresh parsley

1 tablespoon torn or chopped fresh basil, plus more for garnish

4 ounces sharp Cheddar cheese, grated (about 1 cup)

1. In a large skillet, cook the bacon over medium heat, stirring occasionally, until crispy, 6 to 8 minutes, or until the desired crispness. Remove and place on a plate lined with paper towels to cool.

2. Drain off the bacon grease and return the skillet to the stove. Add 2 tablespoons of the butter. Increase the heat to medium-high, add the potatoes and onion, and sauté, stirring occasionally, until the potatoes are browned and the onions are translucent and fragrant, 8 to 10 minutes. Transfer the mixture to the paper towels.

3. In a medium bowl, whisk the eggs and cream until well incorporated. Whisk in the smoked paprika, salt, and pepper.

4. In a small skillet, melt 1 tablespoon of the butter over medium-low heat. Pour one-fourth of the egg mixture into the skillet. Sprinkle with one-fourth each of the bacon, potato/onion mixture, and tomatoes and cook undisturbed for about 4 minutes or until the eggs set. Sprinkle with one-fourth of the chives, parsley, and basil and cook for 1 minute longer to allow the eggs to finish cooking.

5. Sprinkle ¼ cup of the Cheddar over half the omelet. Cover the skillet and cook until the eggs are just cooked through, 30 seconds to 1 minute. Using a spatula, gently fold the omelet in half over the cheese and cook for 1 to 2 minutes.

6. Serve the omelet immediately, garnished with chives and basil. Repeat with the rest of the ingredients to make the remaining 3 omelets.

Makes 4 servings

Kale & Bacon Hash Brown Casserole

prep: *30 minutes*   **cook:** *1 hour 10 minutes*   **cool:** *none*

1 tablespoon unsalted butter, at room temperature

6 slices bacon

½ cup finely diced yellow onion (½ medium)

4 cups lightly packed chopped kale

1 garlic clove, minced

12 large eggs

1 cup whole milk

1 tablespoon Dijon mustard

6 ounces mozzarella cheese, shredded (about 1½ cups)

6 ounces Gruyère cheese, shredded (about 1½ cups)

One 20-ounce bag frozen hash browns, thawed and patted dry

1 teaspoon kosher salt

½ teaspoon freshly ground black pepper

1. Preheat the oven to 350°F. Grease a 9 × 13-inch baking dish with the butter.

2. In a large skillet, cook the bacon over medium-low heat until crispy, 8 to 10 minutes. Transfer the bacon to a plate lined with paper towels and set aside. When cool enough to handle, chop into roughly ¼-inch pieces.

3. Pour off all but 2 tablespoons of the bacon grease from the pan. Set the skillet over medium-high heat, add the onion, and sauté until soft and lightly browned, about 4 minutes. Add the kale and garlic and sauté until the garlic is tender and fragrant, another 3 minutes. Remove from the heat.

4. Add the chopped bacon to the onion/kale mixture.

5. In a large bowl, whisk together the eggs, milk, and mustard. Add ½ cup of the mozzarella, ½ cup of the Gruyère, the hash browns, salt, and pepper. Mix well.

6. Stir the kale mixture into the eggs, then pour into the buttered dish. Top evenly with the remaining mozzarella and Gruyère. Cover with foil.

7. Transfer to the oven and bake for 45 minutes. Remove the foil and bake, uncovered, for 15 minutes, until the top is lightly browned and bubbly.

8. Serve hot.

9. Store in an airtight container in the refrigerator for 3 to 5 days.

Makes 8 to 10 servings

Table Skillet Porridge

prep: *10 minutes*   **cook:** *under 15 minutes*   **cool:** *5 minutes*

3 cups whole milk, or substitute any nut milk

2½ cups rolled oats

1½ teaspoons ground cinnamon

½ teaspoon kosher salt

½ cup pecans

3 tablespoons honey

16 ounces fresh seasonal berries (such as strawberries, blueberries, or blackberries) or dried cranberries

1. In a medium saucepan, combine the milk, 3 cups water, the oats, cinnamon, and salt. Bring to a boil over high heat, then reduce the heat to low, cover, and simmer, stirring occasionally, until thick, about 5 minutes. Remove from the heat and let cool slightly, about 5 minutes.

2. Meanwhile, in a small dry skillet, toast the pecans over medium-high heat, stirring constantly, until fragrant, 3 to 5 minutes. Remove from the skillet and set aside.

3. Divide the oatmeal evenly among bowls and top with a drizzle of honey, the toasted pecans, and fresh berries.

Makes 6 to 8 servings

Bacon Cheddar Cups

prep: *40 minutes*   **cook:** *15 minutes*   **cool:** *5 minutes*

8 slices bacon

Cooking spray

6 large eggs

1 cup cottage cheese

4 ounces Cheddar cheese,
   grated (about 1 cup)

½ teaspoon garlic powder

½ teaspoon onion powder

1 teaspoon ground white
   pepper

1. Preheat the oven to 400°F.

2. Arrange the bacon slices on a sheet pan. Bake until crispy, 20 to 25 minutes. Line a second baking sheet with paper towels and transfer the bacon to the paper towels to drain. When cool enough to handle, chop the bacon.

3. Reduce the oven temperature to 350°F.

4. Spray 12 cups of a muffin tin lightly with cooking spray.

5. In a large bowl, whisk together the eggs and cottage cheese. Stir in the Cheddar, chopped bacon, garlic powder, onion powder, and pepper until just combined.

6. Using a ¼-cup measure, scoop the mixture into the muffin cups. (They should be three-quarters full.)

7. Bake until the cups are creamy in the center and have risen, about 15 minutes.

8. Let cool for 5 minutes before serving.

9. Store in an airtight container in the refrigerator for up to 4 days.

Makes 6 servings

Skillet Potato Hash

prep: *15 minutes*   **cook:** *35 minutes*   **cool:** *none*

1 pound loose pork sausage

4 tablespoons (½ stick) unsalted butter

1½ pounds russet potatoes, unpeeled, cut into ½-inch dice

⅓ cup diced white onion

½ cup diced red bell pepper

½ cup diced green bell pepper

½ cup diced yellow bell pepper

½ jalapeño, minced (about 2 tablespoons)

2 garlic cloves, minced

1 teaspoon kosher salt

½ teaspoon freshly ground black pepper

½ teaspoon paprika

4 ounces Cheddar cheese, grated (about 1 cup)

1. In a large cast-iron skillet, cook the sausage over medium-high heat, stirring often, until thoroughly cooked and browned, about 10 minutes. Transfer to a plate lined with paper towels and drain any excess grease from the pan.

2. Reduce the heat to medium and melt the butter. Add the potatoes and cook, stirring occasionally, until tender and browned, 15 to 17 minutes.

3. Stir in the onion, bell peppers, jalapeño, garlic, salt, black pepper, and paprika and cook, stirring constantly, until the onion and peppers are softened, about 5 minutes. Stir in the sausage, top with the Cheddar, cover the pan, and cook until the cheese is melted, about 2 minutes. Serve hot.

4. Store in an airtight container in the refrigerator for up to 2 days. To reheat, microwave for 2 to 3 minutes, stirring after every minute.

Makes 6 to 8 servings

CHAPTER FOUR

Soups
&
Salads

A MEDLEY OF INGREDIENTS EACH

PLAY THEIR PART IN COMING

TOGETHER TO CREATE SOMETHING

DISTINCTLY DELICIOUS

Spinach Tortellini Soup

prep: *15 minutes*   **cook:** *20 minutes*   **cool:** *none*

The tortellini add a lot of substance to this soup, making it a great all-in-one dinner. This version is my favorite combination of flavors, but it can easily be tailored based on your own palate and what's in season in your area. For instance, you can swap the spinach for really any green that you prefer. If you want a heartier base, add more roasted tomatoes, or for a lighter consistency, try increasing the chicken broth. The best part? Almost any combination will yield really great leftovers.

1 tablespoon unsalted butter

½ medium onion, cut into medium dice

1 tablespoon minced garlic

6 cups (1½ quarts) chicken broth

One 14.5-ounce can diced fire-roasted tomatoes

½ teaspoon Italian seasoning

One 9-ounce package cheese tortellini

One 14.5-ounce can cannellini beans, rinsed well and drained

6 cups baby spinach

2 tablespoons chopped fresh parsley

2 tablespoons chopped fresh basil

Kosher salt and freshly ground black pepper

Juice of ½ lemon

1 cup shaved Parmesan cheese (about 4 ounces)

1 loaf French bread, for serving

1. In a large soup pot, melt the butter over medium-high heat. Add the onion and garlic and sauté, stirring constantly, until the onion is soft and tender, 3 to 4 minutes.

2. Add the broth, tomatoes, and Italian seasoning and bring to a rolling boil. Add the tortellini and beans and cook until the tortellini are cooked through, about 2 minutes.

3. Reduce the heat to medium and add the spinach, parsley, basil, and salt and pepper to taste and stir until the spinach is just wilted, 1 to 2 minutes. Squeeze the lemon juice over the soup.

4. Ladle into bowls, sprinkle with the Parmesan, and serve immediately with torn bread for dipping.

5. Store in an airtight container in the refrigerator for 3 to 4 days or in the freezer for up to 2 months. Let the soup thaw before reheating.

Makes 6 servings

French Lentil Soup

prep: *15 minutes*   **cook:** *1 hour 25 minutes*   **cool:** *none*

It's not easy to find this soup on restaurant menus or in the canned soup aisle at the grocery store, which makes it a special one to make at home, and ideal for ushering in the cooler autumn months. The first soup of the season always feels like a special day in our house—a subtle signal that the season is changing and that our rhythms will soon change along with it.

3 tablespoons unsalted butter

2 cups diced yellow onion (about 1 large)

2 cups diced carrots (about 3)

1¼ cups diced celery (about 3 stalks)

3 smoked ham hocks (about 1½ pounds)

6 cups (1½ quarts) chicken broth

1 cup French green lentils

4 bay leaves

1 teaspoon celery salt

1 teaspoon freshly ground black pepper, plus more to taste

2 tablespoons apple cider vinegar

1 tablespoon fresh thyme leaves

Kosher salt

1. In a large soup pot, melt the butter over medium-high heat. Add the onion, carrots, and celery and cook, stirring often, until tender, about 10 minutes.

2. Add the ham hocks and broth and bring to a slow boil. Add the lentils and stir. Add the bay leaves, celery salt, pepper, vinegar, thyme, and salt to taste and bring the soup to a boil, stirring occasionally.

3. Reduce the heat to medium-low, cover, and cook until the lentils are tender, about 1 hour.

4. Remove the ham hocks and bay leaves. Discard the bay leaves. Shred the meat from the ham hocks and return to the pot (discard the bones, skin, and cartilage). Add more pepper to taste.

5. Serve hot.

6. Store in an airtight container in the refrigerator for up to 5 days, or in the freezer for up to 1 month.

Makes 4 to 6 servings

Creamy Chicken Poblano Soup

prep: *20 minutes*   **cook:** *1 hour 10 minutes*   **cool:** *none*

I've heard it said that food with a story tastes different. For Chip and me, this soup always takes us back to one of our first dates. We went to a restaurant in Dallas and both ordered the chicken poblano soup—not because it was familiar to either of us, but because we had heard that it was the dish the restaurant was known for. Honestly, it was the best soup either of us had ever had. That restaurant and soup became a favorite go-to, and even though the restaurant has since closed, Chip and I still talk about those early days and that chicken poblano soup. This recipe is a nod to the memories of our first dates.

8 tablespoons (1 stick) unsalted butter

2 cups small-diced onion (about 1 large)

4 celery stalks, cut into medium dice

3 carrots, cut into medium dice

2 garlic cloves, minced

3 medium poblano peppers, seeded and cut into medium dice

1½ teaspoons kosher salt

½ teaspoon freshly ground black pepper

1 teaspoon ground cumin

¼ teaspoon dried thyme

8 cups (2 quarts) chicken broth

2 cups heavy cream

3 cups shredded cooked chicken breast (home-roasted or rotisserie chicken)

¼ cup chopped fresh cilantro

Tortilla strips and sliced radishes, for garnish

1. In a large soup pot, melt the butter over medium-high heat. Add the onion, celery, carrots, garlic, and poblanos and sauté, stirring often, until tender, 12 to 15 minutes. Add the salt, pepper, cumin, and thyme and sauté until caramelized and fragrant, 3 to 5 minutes longer.

2. Add the broth and cream, bring to a simmer, then reduce the heat to medium-low and cook, stirring often, for 15 to 20 minutes to meld the flavors.

3. Use an immersion blender to carefully blend the soup until smooth. (Alternatively, let cool slightly and, working in batches as necessary, process in a stand blender until smooth, filling the blender no more than half full and removing the lid slowly after blending. Pour the soup back into the pot.)

4. Add the chicken and simmer for 15 to 30 minutes to meld the flavors to your liking. Stir in the cilantro.

5. Serve warm, garnished with tortilla strips and sliced radishes.

6. Store in an airtight container in the refrigerator for up to 3 days or in the freezer for up to 1 month.

Makes 6 to 8 servings

French Onion Soup

prep: *15 minutes*   **cook:** *1 hour*   **cool:** *none*

8 tablespoons (1 stick) unsalted butter

8 cups sliced yellow onion (about 3 medium)

2 garlic cloves, minced

4 thyme sprigs

2 bay leaves

¼ cup sherry (or white wine vinegar or additional broth)

6 cups (1½ quarts) beef broth

½ teaspoon kosher salt

¼ teaspoon freshly ground black pepper

8 to 16 crostini, homemade (page 49) or store-bought

8 ounces Gruyère cheese, shredded (about 2 cups)

1. In a large soup pot, melt the butter over medium-high heat. Add the onion and sauté, stirring occasionally, until it begins to caramelize, 20 to 25 minutes. Add the garlic, thyme, and bay leaves and cook until fragrant, 2 to 3 minutes. Add the sherry and stir to loosen any browned bits on the bottom of the pot. Let simmer until almost all the liquid has evaporated, 1 to 2 minutes. Add the broth, bring the mixture to a low boil, and boil for 2 to 3 minutes. Reduce the heat to medium-low, stir in the salt and pepper, and simmer for 15 to 20 minutes to meld the flavors.

2. Position a rack 4 to 5 inches from the heat and turn the broiler to low if possible. (If a low setting is not available, then position the rack 6 to 8 inches from the heat.)

3. Discard the bay leaves. Ladle the soup into eight 12-ounce ovenproof bowls and place them on a sheet pan. Top each bowl with a crostini or two and cover with the shredded Gruyère.

4. Broil until the Gruyère begins to bubble and brown, about 5 minutes. Watch carefully; the cheese can burn quickly.

5. Serve immediately.

Makes 8 servings

Chicken Soup

WITH HOMEMADE NOODLES

prep: *15 minutes*   **cook:** *under 40 minutes*   **cool:** *none*

Homemade Noodles (page 33)

4 tablespoons (½ stick) unsalted butter

½ cup diced onion (about ½ medium)

2 celery stalks, diced

3 carrots, diced

½ teaspoon kosher salt

¼ teaspoon ground white pepper

8 cups (2 quarts) chicken broth

4 cups shredded cooked chicken breast (home-roasted or rotisserie chicken)

1 tablespoon chopped fresh parsley

1. Make the noodles as directed and cover with a damp cloth or paper towel.

2. In a large soup pot, melt the butter over medium heat. Add the onion and sauté until softened, about 5 minutes. Add the celery and carrots and cook until soft and tender, 5 to 8 minutes. Stir in the salt and pepper.

3. Add the broth and bring to a boil over medium-high heat. Reduce to a simmer, carefully add the noodles, and simmer until they are cooked through, 15 to 20 minutes.

4. Add the chicken and simmer 5 minutes to warm through. Sprinkle with the parsley and serve.

5. Store in an airtight container in the refrigerator for up to 3 days, or in the freezer for up to 1 month.

Makes 8 to 10 servings

Classic Minestrone

prep: *15 minutes*   **cook:** *40 minutes*   **cool:** *none*

3 tablespoons olive oil

5 garlic cloves, minced

½ white onion (about 1 medium), cut into small dice

1 medium zucchini, cut into medium dice

1 medium yellow squash, cut into medium dice

2 large carrots, cut into medium dice

3 celery stalks, cut into medium dice

One 14.5-ounce can crushed tomatoes

One 14.5-ounce can diced tomatoes

4 cups (1 quart) chicken broth

4 cups (1 quart) vegetable broth

1 teaspoon dried basil

1 teaspoon kosher salt

1 teaspoon freshly ground black pepper

1 cup large or small shell pasta

One 15.5-ounce can kidney beans, rinsed well and drained

One 15-ounce can cannellini beans, rinsed well and drained

3 cups baby spinach

½ cup grated Parmesan cheese (about 2 ounces)

3 tablespoons chopped fresh basil

1. In a large soup pot, heat the olive oil over medium heat. Add the garlic and cook until fragrant, about 1 minute. Add the onion, zucchini, yellow squash, carrots, and celery and cook, stirring constantly, until the vegetables are tender, about 5 minutes.

2. Stir in the crushed tomatoes, diced tomatoes, chicken broth, vegetable broth, dried basil, salt, and pepper. Bring to a boil over medium-high heat, reduce the heat to medium-low, and simmer for 20 minutes, until the flavors are melded.

3. Add the pasta and cook until tender, about 12 minutes. Add the beans and spinach and cook until the spinach is wilted, 1 to 2 minutes.

4. Ladle into bowls and top with the Parmesan and fresh basil.

5. Store in an airtight container in the refrigerator for up to 5 days, or in the freezer for up to 1 month.

Makes 8 servings

Mom's Seaweed Soup

prep: *15 minutes*   **cook:** *under 1 hour*   **cool:** *none*

It is Korean custom to make seaweed soup for a new mom after she's given birth because it's packed with all kinds of nutrients and a variety of protective antioxidants that are so healthy for the body. As soon as one of my sisters or I am home from the hospital after having a baby, my mom shows up with a big batch of soup. And because it has become a staple dish of my mom's, it is something my kids have grown to love. The memories attached to it have made it such a nostalgic meal for all of us, so much so that I've actually started to commission my mom to make our family a big batch about once every season, which I'll share with the kids (with a little reluctance, if I'm being honest). The texture of the soup is something you have to get familiar with, but once you do, the rich flavor becomes this experience that's almost impossible to put into words. Just trust me on this one—and if it turns out that the taste isn't for you, at least you'll know it's doing great things for your body.

1 cup torn wakame

1 tablespoon toasted sesame oil

1½ pounds beef tenderloin, cut into ½-inch cubes

¾ teaspoon kosher salt

½ teaspoon freshly ground black pepper

½ teaspoon minced garlic

1 tablespoon jarred concentrated beef stock base

½ cup chopped green onions

2 cups uncooked sticky rice

Sesame seeds, for garnish

1. Place the wakame in a medium bowl and cover with warm water. Let sit at room temperature until fully rehydrated and pliable, about 5 minutes. Drain and set aside.

2. In a large soup pot or Dutch oven, heat the sesame oil over medium-high heat. Add the beef, ½ teaspoon of the salt, and the pepper and cook, stirring occasionally, until the beef is lightly browned, 8 to 12 minutes. Add the garlic and cook, stirring constantly, until softened and fragrant, about 1 minute.

3. Stir in 8 cups water and the beef stock base. Bring to a boil over high heat, then add the wakame and ¼ cup of the green onions. Reduce the heat to medium-low and simmer, stirring occasionally, for 45 minutes to concentrate the flavors. Stir in the remaining ¼ teaspoon salt.

4. Meanwhile, cook the rice according to the package directions. Cover and keep warm.

5. Divide the rice evenly among six bowls. Ladle the soup over the rice and sprinkle with the remaining ¼ cup green onions. Garnish with sesame seeds and serve.

6. Store in an airtight container in the refrigerator for up to 3 days.

Makes 6 servings

Avocado Grapefruit Salad

prep: *25 minutes*   **cook:** *none*   **cool:** *none*

This is a simple salad that I'll throw together when I want something bright, citrusy, and full of flavor. The ingredients make for a beautiful blend of taste and color that I never tire of. I like to top it off with a small pour of olive oil and a pinch of flaky sea salt.

3 large Ruby Red or other grapefruit

2 heads butterhead or Bibb lettuce, leaves torn (about 8 cups)

3 large avocados, pitted, peeled, and thinly sliced

1 tablespoon honey

1 tablespoon fresh lime juice

2 tablespoons olive oil

½ teaspoon kosher salt

¼ teaspoon freshly ground black pepper

1 tablespoon chopped fresh parsley

1 tablespoon chopped fresh cilantro

Flaky sea salt, such as Maldon

1. Peel the grapefruit and use a sharp knife to release the segments from their membranes. Do this over a bowl to catch the juices. Measure out 2 tablespoons juice to use in the dressing.

2. Spread the torn lettuce on a large platter. Arrange the grapefruit sections and avocado slices over the lettuce.

3. To make the dressing: In a medium bowl, whisk together the grapefruit juice, honey, lime juice, 1 tablespoon of the olive oil, the salt, and pepper.

4. Drizzle the salad with the dressing. Sprinkle with the herbs and flaky sea salt to taste and drizzle with the remaining 1 tablespoon olive oil. Serve immediately.

Makes 6 servings

Sweet Kale Salad

WITH POPPY SEED DRESSING

prep: *15 minutes, plus 15 minutes chilling*   **cook:** *none*   **cool:** *none*

poppy seed dressing

¼ cup plus 1 tablespoon sugar

⅓ cup white wine vinegar

1 teaspoon mustard powder

1½ teaspoons kosher salt

½ teaspoon ground white pepper

⅓ cup grated yellow onion

¾ cup canola oil

¼ cup olive oil

1 tablespoon poppy seeds

salad

2 bunches kale or 10 ounces curly kale leaves

½ cup dried cranberries

1 cup shredded carrots

¼ cup sunflower seeds

1. To make the poppy seed dressing: In a blender or food processor, add the sugar, vinegar, mustard powder, salt, pepper, and onion and pulse to combine, about 30 seconds.

2. With the machine running, slowly add the canola and olive oils until smooth, 2 to 3 minutes.

3. Add the poppy seeds and blend just until combined.

4. Cover and refrigerate until ready to use. (Store in an airtight container in the refrigerator for up to 1 month.)

5. To make the salad: Rinse and dry the kale, unless using prepackaged. Remove the midribs and slice the kale into thin strips.

6. Toss the kale in a large bowl with the cranberries, carrots, and sunflower seeds. Pour ⅓ cup of the dressing over the kale mixture and use your hands to toss and coat well, massaging the kale with your hands. (Reserve the remaining dressing for another use.)

7. Refrigerate for 15 minutes before serving.

8. Store in an airtight container in the refrigerator for up to 2 days.

Makes 4 servings, about 2 cups dressing

TIP: *Top with chicken or roasted salmon for a hearty dish. Dressing tastes better if you prepare it the night before. Plus, it saves you time the next day!*

Salade Niçoise

prep: *20 minutes*   **cook:** *10 minutes*   **cool:** *10 minutes*

Pronounced "nee-swaaz," this protein-heavy salad originated in France and remains a French bistro staple. The original recipe has been built upon and changed a hundred times over, but the basics remain rich in protein and vegetables. This recipe is easily customizable—take out the hard-boiled eggs or capers if you don't like them, add your favorite greens, and so on. The Weeknight Salmon is my favorite protein to add here, but it's also delicious with a simple roasted chicken.

1½ teaspoons kosher salt

½ pound small red or new potatoes

8 ounces green beans, ends snapped

1 head romaine lettuce, cut crosswise into 1-inch strips

8 ounces Weeknight Salmon (page 235), flaked

4 hard-boiled eggs, halved

2 tablespoons drained capers

¼ cup kalamata olives

2 tablespoons red wine vinegar

1 tablespoon Dijon mustard

½ teaspoon freshly ground black pepper

½ cup extra virgin olive oil

1. Set up a large bowl of ice and water. Bring a large pot of water to a boil over high heat with 1 teaspoon of the salt. Add the potatoes and boil until you can easily pierce them with a knife, about 10 minutes. Add the green beans and boil for 1 minute, until the green beans are bright green and the potatoes are cooked through.

2. With a slotted spoon, remove the potatoes and green beans and place them in the bowl of ice water to stop the cooking process. Let chill for 1 to 2 minutes, drain, and set aside to cool completely. When they are cool enough to handle, halve the potatoes.

3. Spread the lettuce on a large platter and arrange individual sections of the salmon, eggs, capers, olives, and chilled green beans and potatoes over the lettuce.

4. To make the dressing: In a medium bowl, whisk together the vinegar, mustard, remaining ½ teaspoon salt, the pepper, and olive oil until emulsified. Drizzle the dressing over the salad right before serving or serve on the side.

Makes 4 servings

Mexican Party Salad

prep: *25 minutes*   **cook:** *under 10 minutes*   **cool:** *none*

1 teaspoon olive oil

1 pound ground beef
(80% lean)

2 teaspoons ground cumin

1 teaspoon chili powder

1 teaspoon garlic salt

½ teaspoon freshly ground
black pepper

1 head iceberg lettuce, cored
and roughly chopped

¾ cup halved grape tomatoes

One 15-ounce can kidney
beans, rinsed well and
drained

4 ounces Cheddar cheese,
grated (about 1 cup)

⅔ cup bottled French
dressing

1 cup broken tortilla chips

1 large avocado, pitted,
peeled, and cut into
medium dice, for garnish

Roughly chopped fresh
cilantro, for garnish
(optional)

Lime slices, for serving
(optional)

1. In a large skillet, heat the oil over medium-high heat. Add the ground beef, breaking it up well with a wooden spoon. Sprinkle with the cumin, chili powder, garlic salt, and pepper and cook, stirring often, until cooked through, about 5 minutes.

2. Remove the skillet from the heat and drain off the grease.

3. Place the lettuce in a large bowl. Add the tomatoes, kidney beans, Cheddar, and ground beef. Drizzle the dressing over the salad and toss to combine well. Add the chips and give one last toss.

4. Garnish with the avocado and cilantro and lime (if using). Serve immediately.

Makes 4 servings

Asian Salad

WITH SWEET VINAIGRETTE

prep: *15 minutes*   **cook:** *under 15 minutes*   **cool:** *10 minutes*

The toasted almonds—tossed with honey and then coated with sesame seeds—are the real stars here. They're delicious enough on their own that I like to make an extra half-batch just to snack on. If you want to make this salad as your main dish, it pairs well with a protein like shrimp, chicken, or seared beef.

dressing

½ cup rice vinegar

2 tablespoons olive oil

1 tablespoon light brown sugar

½ teaspoon kosher salt

salad

Cooking spray

2 cups whole raw almonds

1 teaspoon olive oil

3 tablespoons honey

½ teaspoon coarse salt

¼ cup sesame seeds

One 11-ounce can mandarin oranges

2 heads butterhead or Bibb lettuce, torn into large pieces (about 8 cups)

1 cup canned chow mein noodles

1. To make the dressing: In a screw-top jar, combine the vinegar, oil, 1 tablespoon water, the brown sugar, and salt. Screw on the lid and shake well.

2. Preheat the oven to 375°F. Spray a sheet pan with cooking spray.

3. To make the salad: In a large bowl, toss the almonds with the olive oil. Add the honey and coarse salt and toss to combine.

4. Spread the almonds evenly on the sheet pan and roast until toasted, about 12 minutes, stirring every 2 to 3 minutes. Remove from the oven and sprinkle with the sesame seeds. Stir to coat. Let stand until cool, 10 minutes, then break any clumps of almonds apart.

5. Reserving the liquid, drain the mandarins and spread them on a paper towel to absorb excess moisture. Add the reserved liquid to the dressing jar and shake well.

6. In a large bowl, combine the lettuce, mandarins, almonds, and chow mein noodles.

7. Toss the salad with ¼ cup of the dressing and serve the remaining dressing on the side.

8. Store the dressing in an airtight container in the refrigerator for 4 to 5 days.

Makes 6 servings

CHAPTER FIVE

Appetizers & Starters

ANTICIPATION GIVES WAY TO

FRUITION AND IT SETS THE

COURSE FOR WHAT'S TO COME

Puff Pastry

WITH BRIE AND JAM

prep: *15 minutes*   **cook:** *under 35 minutes*   **cool:** *none*

There are so many aspects of this dish—the warm bread, sweet jam, and 10-minute prep—that make it a favorite of mine to serve at home or bring to a dinner party. Plus, it's incredibly versatile. I'll serve it with fig jam around the holidays and then swap in a peach or raspberry preserve in the spring or summertime.

1 sheet frozen puff pastry, thawed

One 8-ounce wheel Brie cheese

4 tablespoons good-quality jam of your choice

1 cup walnut halves

2 teaspoons olive oil

1 tablespoon light brown sugar

1 tablespoon garlic salt

1 teaspoon minced mixed fresh herbs, such as chives, thyme, or rosemary

Crackers, for serving

1. Preheat the oven to 350°F.

2. Open the pastry sheet on a baking sheet and place the Brie in the center. Top the Brie with 2 tablespoons of the jam. (It doesn't matter if the jam runs off the center.) Bring the pastry up around the Brie and pleat the edges, pressing to envelop the sides of the Brie. Be sure to seal any openings to prevent the jam from seeping out while baking.

3. Bake until the pastry is lightly browned and the Brie is very soft, 30 to 35 minutes.

4. Meanwhile, in a large skillet, combine the walnuts, olive oil, brown sugar, and garlic salt and cook over medium heat, stirring often, until the walnuts have a golden buttered look with some browned and darker bits, 5 to 7 minutes. Set aside.

5. Transfer the baked Brie to a serving plate. Top with the remaining 2 tablespoons jam, the walnuts, and the fresh herbs.

6. Serve immediately with crackers (this will not keep well).

Makes 6 to 8 servings

Prosciutto-Wrapped Apples

prep: *25 minutes*   **cook:** *none*   **cool:** *none*

Cooking is always most enjoyable when I feel like I am tapping in to some creative outlet—when food becomes an art form of its own, not just a necessity for our survival. If you were to deconstruct this recipe, you'd see that it's made up of only a few really basic foods. But when you put them together, they create a taste so delicious it makes you wonder if there's some magic ingredient holding it all together.

2 large Honeycrisp apples or 3 sweet apples, such as Gala, unpeeled and cored

2 cups loosely packed baby or standard arugula

8 ounces sharp white Cheddar cheese, cut into twenty 3 × 1-inch slices

Two 3-ounce packages thinly sliced prosciutto, torn into strips

¼ cup balsamic glaze

Kosher salt and freshly ground black pepper

1. Cut the apples into a total of 20 wedges (10 wedges per large apple or 6 to 7 per smaller apple).

2. Layer a few arugula leaves on an apple wedge, then top with a Cheddar slice. Wrap the stack with a strip of prosciutto and place on a platter. Repeat to make the rest of the wrapped apples.

3. Drizzle the wrapped apples with the balsamic glaze and season to taste with salt and pepper. Serve immediately.

Makes 6 to 8 servings

Bruschetta Trio

prep: *10 minutes*   **cook:** *25 minutes for steak*   **cool:** *5 minutes for steak*

12 to 16 Crostini (page 49)

prosciutto & brie

3 ounces thinly sliced
   prosciutto, torn into strips

4 ounces cold Brie cheese,
   cut into 12 to 16 thin slices

¼ cup peach preserves

1 teaspoon fresh thyme leaves

Kosher salt and freshly ground
   black pepper

caprese

8 ounces fresh mozzarella
   balls, cut into twelve
   ¼-inch-thick slices

12 to 16 cherry tomatoes
   (about 4 ounces), halved

½ tablespoon olive oil

Kosher salt and freshly ground
   black pepper

12 to 16 small fresh basil
   leaves (or 3 or 4 large
   leaves, thinly sliced)

steak & arugula

1 cup cherry tomatoes, halved

½ tablespoon balsamic vinegar

1 tablespoon olive oil

10-ounce New York strip
   steak, 1½ inches thick

Kosher salt and freshly ground
   black pepper

1 cup arugula

¼ cup blue cheese crumbles
   (optional)

Make the crostini as directed and set aside. Prepare one of the topping options. Follow the directions in the individual topping recipes to prepare and assemble the bruschetta.

to make the prosciutto & brie

To assemble the bruschetta: Fold the prosciutto strips artfully on top of each crostini. Top with a slice of Brie and a small spoonful of preserves. Sprinkle the bruschetta with the thyme and salt and pepper to taste.

to make the caprese

To assemble the bruschetta: Top each crostini with 1 mozzarella slice and 2 tomato halves. Drizzle evenly with the olive oil and season to taste with salt and pepper. Top with the fresh basil.

to make the steak & arugula

1. Preheat the oven to 425°F.

2. Arrange the tomatoes on a sheet pan and drizzle them with the balsamic and ½ tablespoon of the olive oil. Toss to coat. Season with salt and pepper and roast until caramelized, about 20 minutes.

3. Meanwhile, season both sides of the steak with salt and pepper. Heat an ovenproof medium skillet over medium-high heat and add ¾ teaspoon of the olive oil. Add the steak and sear until browned on both sides, 2 to 3 minutes per side. Transfer the skillet to the oven and roast for 4 to 6 minutes for medium doneness. Remove the steak from the oven and set it aside to rest for 3 to 5 minutes before slicing into very thin strips.

4. In a small bowl, toss the arugula with the remaining ¾ teaspoon olive oil and season with salt and pepper. Toss to lightly coat.

5. To assemble the bruschetta: Layer the crostini with the arugula, sliced steak, and roasted tomatoes. If desired, top with the blue cheese crumbles.

Each makes 6 to 8 servings

Arancini

WITH JO'S MARINARA SAUCE

prep: *30 minutes, plus at least 1 hour chilling*   **cook:** *under 30 minutes*   **cool:** *none*

32 ounces (1 quart) chicken stock or store-bought chicken broth

5 tablespoons unsalted butter

½ cup small-diced yellow onion (about ½ medium)

1 garlic clove, minced

1 cup Arborio rice

½ teaspoon kosher salt

¼ teaspoon freshly ground black pepper

4 ounces Parmesan cheese, grated (about 1 cup)

½ cup heavy cream

½ teaspoon grated lemon zest

1 teaspoon fresh lemon juice

2 cups panko bread crumbs

1 cup all-purpose flour

3 large eggs

Kosher salt and freshly ground black pepper

Canola oil, for deep-frying (about 6 cups)

2 cups Jo's Marinara Sauce (page 36), for serving

1. In a large pot, bring the chicken stock to a simmer.

2. In large saucepan or Dutch oven, melt 3 tablespoons of the butter over medium-high heat. Add the onion and sauté, stirring, until translucent, 5 to 8 minutes. Add the garlic and sauté 10 to 15 seconds, until tender. Reduce the heat to medium, add the rice, and cook for 1 to 2 minutes, stirring constantly. Season with the salt and pepper.

3. Ladle 1 cup of the stock into the rice mixture and stir constantly until the rice soaks up all the liquid, about 5 minutes. Continue adding the stock 1 cup at a time, stirring constantly and letting the rice soak up the liquid before adding more. When all the stock has been added, cook, stirring constantly, until all the liquid is absorbed and the risotto is thickened, 3 to 5 minutes.

4. Remove from the heat and add the Parmesan, cream, lemon zest, lemon juice, and remaining 2 tablespoons butter. Stir until well combined.

5. Line a sheet pan with parchment paper. Spread the risotto out on it to cool for 30 minutes, then cover with plastic wrap and refrigerate until fully chilled, for at least 1 hour.

6. Pour the panko and flour into two medium bowls. Whisk the eggs in a third bowl and season with ½ teaspoon salt and ½ teaspoon pepper.

7. Shape the risotto into 1½-inch balls, using gloves or lightly spraying your hands with olive oil to keep the balls from sticking. You will have 18 to 20 risotto balls. Freeze the risotto balls on a sheet pan for 10 minutes.

8. Dredge a risotto ball in the flour, coating it well, then dip it in the egg mixture, letting the excess egg drip back into the bowl. Roll the ball in panko to coat it well. Repeat to coat the rest and refrigerate while the oil heats.

9. Pour 2 inches of oil into a large pot. Have ready a wire rack lined with paper towels. Heat the oil to 350°F on a deep-fry thermometer.

10. Working in batches, use a slotted spoon or spider to lower a few arancini at a time into the hot oil. Do not add more than can float freely in the hot oil. Fry until deep golden brown, 4 to 6 minutes. Drain them on the paper towel–lined rack and season with salt and pepper to taste. Repeat to fry all the arancini.

11. Serve hot with marinara or divide among plates and cover with the sauce.

Makes 18 to 20 arancini

Pesto Burrata

WITH ROASTED CHERRY TOMATOES

prep: *15 minutes*   **cook:** *under 20 minutes*   **cool:** *none*

2 cups cherry tomatoes, halved

1 tablespoon olive oil, plus 1 teaspoon for drizzling

½ teaspoon kosher salt, plus more to taste

¼ teaspoon freshly ground black pepper, plus more to taste

Two 8-ounce containers burrata cheese (or four 4-ounce balls)

3 tablespoons pesto, homemade (see page 37) or store-bought

Crostini (page 49), for serving

1. Preheat the oven to 450°F. Line a baking sheet with foil.

2. On the prepared baking sheet, toss the cherry tomatoes with the 1 tablespoon olive oil, salt, and pepper. Roast for 18 to 20 minutes, until browned and soft. Set aside to cool while you prepare the rest of the dish.

3. Remove the burrata from the water and pat dry with a paper towel.

4. Carefully slice each burrata into halves or quarters and place on a serving platter or in a large serving bowl.

5. Drizzle with the remaining 1 teaspoon of olive oil and pesto. Sprinkle with the tomatoes and season to taste with salt and pepper.

6. Serve with the crostini.

Makes 4 to 6 servings

Roasted Garlic Bulbs

prep: *15 minutes*   **cook:** *under 1 hour 10 minutes*   **cool:** *none*

It had been a long day of travel for work when I checked into my hotel late one night, only to realize that I hadn't eaten dinner. I called a few people on our team to see if anyone wanted to walk down with me to the hotel restaurant. At our server's recommendation, we ordered a plate of roasted garlic bulbs for a starter. I had no idea that garlic, when roasted, would spread like butter on toasted bread. It was everything I never knew I wanted, and when it came time to develop recipes for this book, I thought there was a good chance you might feel the same.

8 large garlic heads (elephant garlic, if possible)

4 tablespoons olive oil

4 tablespoons (½ stick) unsalted butter, cut into 8 slices

1 teaspoon fresh thyme leaves

¼ teaspoon chopped fresh rosemary

¼ teaspoon flaky sea salt, such as Maldon

¼ teaspoon freshly ground black pepper

3 tablespoons grated Parmesan cheese (optional)

Torn or sliced baguette or sourdough bread, for serving

1. Preheat the oven to 400°F.

2. Using a large sharp knife, cut the top ¼ inch of the garlic heads off to expose the cloves, leaving the whole heads intact.

3. Place the garlic heads cut sides up, touching one another, in a 9- or 10-inch cast-iron skillet. Drizzle with 3 tablespoons of the olive oil and top each with a slice of butter. Sprinkle the thyme, rosemary, salt, and pepper on top.

4. Cover the skillet tightly with foil to keep in the moisture. Transfer to the oven and roast until the garlic is very soft, about 1 hour. Remove from the oven and carefully open the foil to avoid the steam. If using the Parmesan, sprinkle it over the garlic.

5. Return to the oven and roast, uncovered, until the tops begin to brown, 5 to 8 minutes.

6. Drizzle with the remaining 1 tablespoon olive oil. You can serve the heads of garlic in the skillet or transfer them to a warmed serving platter and pour any pan juices over them.

7. Spread the warm garlic onto torn or sliced bread.

Makes 8 to 10 servings

Ham & Spinach Puffs

prep: *25 minutes*   **cook:** *15 minutes*   **cool:** *5 minutes*

1 package (2 sheets) frozen puff pastry

3 cups chopped fresh baby spinach (about 3 ounces)

½ teaspoon olive oil

⅛ teaspoon kosher salt

¼ teaspoon freshly ground black pepper

Flour, for the work surface

2 tablespoons Dijon mustard

Cooking spray

18 thin slices Black Forest ham (about 9 ounces)

4 ounces Gruyère cheese, grated (about 1 cup)

1. Remove the puff pastry dough from the freezer and take it out of the packaging. Let thaw at room temperature for 15 to 20 minutes, until it unfolds easily, taking care not to tear it.

2. Preheat the oven to 400°F.

3. Meanwhile, in a large bowl, combine the spinach, olive oil, salt, and pepper. Toss to lightly coat. Set aside.

4. Lay out the thawed pastry sheets on a lightly floured work surface and cut each into 9 even squares, for a total of 18.

5. Spread the mustard in a thin layer over each dough square and top with a ham slice, folding the slices as needed to fit.

6. Lightly spray 18 cups of two 12-cup muffin pans with cooking spray (if the pan is not nonstick). Set a prepared dough square into each cup and gently nestle it in. The sides should ruffle. Drop about 2 packed tablespoons of spinach evenly into each cup and top with about 1 tablespoon of Gruyère.

7. Bake until the edges are golden brown, about 15 minutes. Remove the puffs from the pans and let cool for 5 minutes before serving.

8. Store in an airtight container in the refrigerator for up to 3 days. Reheat in a toaster oven.

Makes 18 puffs

Twice-Baked New Potatoes

prep: *20 minutes, with 10 minutes cooling*   **cook:** *20 minutes*   **cool:** *none*

6 small potatoes (about 1 pound total)

⅓ cup sour cream

1½ tablespoons heavy cream

1½ tablespoons unsalted butter, melted

½ teaspoon garlic powder

½ teaspoon onion powder

½ teaspoon freshly ground black pepper

¼ teaspoon kosher salt

4 ounces sharp Cheddar cheese, grated (about 1 cup)

4 slices bacon, cooked until crisp and crumbled

2 tablespoons minced chives

1. In a large pot, combine the potatoes with water to cover by 1 inch. Bring to a boil over high heat and boil until tender and cooked all the way through, about 15 minutes. Drain the potatoes. When cool enough to handle, slice the potatoes in half and set aside on a sheet pan.

2. Using a small spoon, scoop out the potatoes, leaving ¼ inch of the shell intact. Transfer the potato flesh to a medium bowl and add the sour cream, heavy cream, melted butter, garlic powder, onion powder, pepper, and salt. Mix until well combined.

3. Position a rack 5 inches from the heat and preheat the broiler.

4. Scoop the filling back into the potato shells and top with the Cheddar. Broil until the potatoes are browned and the cheese is melted and toasty, 3 to 5 minutes. Top with the bacon and chives and serve right away.

5. Store in an airtight container in the refrigerator for 3 to 5 days. Reheat in a 350°F oven for 20 minutes and serve.

Makes 4 servings

French Onion Dip

prep: *40 minutes*   **cook:** *under 25 minutes*   **cool:** *1 hour*

A friend of mine makes this dip every year for a group of us on New Year's Day, and it is, without fail, one of the first dishes to be completely devoured. It's creamy and delicious and totally worth breaking all your healthy-eating resolutions for.

8 tablespoons (1 stick) unsalted butter

3 large sweet onions, such as Vidalia, cut into ⅛-inch slices

½ cup small-diced shallots (about 2 large)

2 garlic cloves, minced

3 cups sour cream

2 cups mayonnaise, preferably Hellmann's

1 tablespoon celery salt

1 tablespoon Worcestershire

2 teaspoons fresh lemon juice

¼ teaspoon kosher salt

½ teaspoon freshly ground black pepper

1 tablespoon minced chives

1. Depending on the size of the skillet, you may need to sauté in two batches. In a large skillet, melt the butter over medium-high heat until it bubbles. Add the onions and shallots and sauté, stirring occasionally, until golden brown, 20 to 25 minutes. Add the garlic in the last minute of cooking and sauté just until fragrant. Set the pan aside to cool for about 15 minutes, then transfer the onion mixture to a cutting board.

2. Meanwhile, in a large bowl, combine the sour cream, mayonnaise, celery salt, Worcestershire, lemon juice, kosher salt, and pepper. Whisk until well mixed.

3. Chop the cooled onion mixture and add it to the bowl. Fold into the mixture until well incorporated. Cover the bowl and refrigerate for at least 1 hour or up to overnight. Stir again and sprinkle with chives right before serving.

4. Store in an airtight container in the refrigerator for up to 2 days.

Makes about 8 cups

Cheese Balls, Four Ways

prep: *25 minutes, plus 4 hours chilling*   **cook:** *none*   **cool:** *none*

I will always be a believer in the tried-and-true cheese ball. It's the ideal party food: easy to make, easy to travel with, easy to serve—and always a crowd favorite. On weekends, our family typically starts the day with a big breakfast, and we often skip lunch altogether, but these are always a welcome snack that tides everyone over till dinner.

cheese balls

Two 8-ounce blocks cream cheese, at room temperature

8 ounces sharp white Cheddar cheese, grated (about 2 cups)

8 ounces Gouda cheese, shredded (about 2 cups)

3 tablespoons minced sun-dried tomatoes

3 tablespoons chopped fresh dill or basil

1 teaspoon garlic salt

½ teaspoon freshly ground black pepper

coating options

1 cup minced fresh parsley

2 tablespoons freshly cracked black pepper

¼ cup toasted sesame seeds

1 cup walnuts, toasted and finely chopped

1. To make the cheese balls: In a large bowl, combine the cream cheese, Cheddar, Gouda, sun-dried tomatoes, dill, garlic salt, and pepper and mix well. Form the mixture into 2 cheese balls.

2. Choose one or two of the coating options (see Note). Place the coating in a shallow bowl and roll the balls to cover them well.

3. Wrap the balls individually in plastic wrap and refrigerate for at least 4 hours or up to overnight to let the flavors blend. Let the cheese balls sit out at room temperature for 1 hour before serving.

4. Store in an airtight container in the refrigerator for 3 to 5 days.

Makes two 12-ounce cheese balls

NOTE: *If you want to use a different coating for each cheese ball, cut the quantity of the coating ingredients in half.*

Mini Cheese Ball Bites

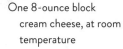

prep: *30 minutes*   **cook:** *none*   **cool:** *none*

One 8-ounce block
  cream cheese, at room
  temperature

2 ounces Cheddar cheese,
  grated (about ½ cup)

¾ cup minced black olives,
  drained and dried with
  paper towels

1 teaspoon onion powder

½ teaspoon garlic salt

½ teaspoon freshly ground
  black pepper

1 cup minced fresh parsley

1 cup roughly chopped pecans
  (optional)

1. In a medium bowl, combine the cream cheese, Cheddar, olives, onion powder, garlic salt, and pepper. Place the parsley on a plate. Place the pecans on a separate plate (if using).

2. Use a melon baller to scoop a tablespoon of the mixture. Roll the ball in your hands to form a perfect sphere, then roll the ball in the parsley (and/or pecans) and place on a serving platter. Repeat to make the rest of the cheese balls.

3. They can be served immediately but taste best if refrigerated at least 4 hours or up to overnight and then left at room temperature for 30 to 60 minutes before serving.

4. Store in an airtight container in the refrigerator for up to 2 days.

Makes 12 to 14 mini cheese balls

charcuterie board

STEP 1 | cheeses

Select cheeses with varying textures to give your board balance and visual interest. A combination of soft, firm, and hard cheeses is a great starting point. From there, it's helpful to incorporate a few options that are easy to dip or scoop onto bread or crackers, in addition to harder cheeses that require a cheese knife.

Soft cheese: Brie, ricotta, feta, panela, blue cheese/Roquefort, Camembert
Firm cheese: Cheddar, Gruyère, Gouda, Monterey Jack, Edam
Hard cheese: Pecorino Romano, aged Gouda, Parmesan

STEP 2 | meats

Utilize different types and cuts of meat to create dimension and movement on the board. Thinly shaved prosciutto and medium-sliced salami are easiest to fold and tuck between cheeses. Pair the meats with your preferred cheese or garnish.

Soppressata salami (whole black peppercorns and garlic)
Calabrese salami (cayenne pepper makes it spicy)
Prosciutto

STEP 3 | crackers

Crackers also contribute to the texture and balance of the board. It's typically best to incorporate the same number of cracker varieties as cheeses. A selection of seeded crackers, thin water crackers, and sheets of lavash that can be torn and spread out across the board to make for a good foundation.

STEP 4 | accoutrements

Add fresh color to your board by incorporating small flowering herbs (like fresh thyme, mint, basil, and lavender), and vegetables to garnish, such as radishes and cherry tomatoes. Fresh honeycomb, seasonal fruits, sauces, and nuts help anchor and bring a little life to your board.

CHAPTER SIX

Side Dishes

LIKE A SUPPORTING CHARACTER,

A GOOD SIDE ALWAYS COMPLEMENTS

THE MAIN ATTRACTION

Cauliflower Couscous

prep: *30 minutes*   **cook:** *15 minutes*   **cool:** *none*

Couscous is typically cooked a little soft for my taste, and while that may very well be the way it's traditionally prepared, I wanted to develop a version for this book that had a bit more of a crunch and freshness to it. Our take is flexible for every season. I'll toss in dried cranberries in the spring and dried apricots in the fall, and it's equally delicious served cold or warm.

½ cup dried cranberries

1 cup boiling water

8 cups cauliflower florets (about 3¾ pounds, from 2 medium heads)

3 tablespoons salted butter

¼ cup thinly sliced shallot (about 1 small)

3 garlic cloves, minced

3 cups finely chopped stemmed kale leaves (about one 5-ounce bunch)

½ cup chopped almonds

1½ teaspoons kosher salt

2 teaspoons sherry vinegar

½ cup chopped green onions

1. In a small heatproof bowl, combine the cranberries and boiling water. Let stand until the fruit is softened, about 10 minutes. Drain and set aside.

2. Meanwhile, working in batches of about 2 cups of florets, process the cauliflower in a food processor until very finely chopped (about the size of couscous), about 10 seconds. Process any large remaining pieces with the next batch. Pour into a bowl and repeat with all the cauliflower.

3. In a large skillet, melt 2 tablespoons of the butter over medium-high heat. Add the shallot and garlic and cook, stirring frequently, until slightly softened, about 1½ minutes. Stir in the cauliflower and spread it into a single layer. Cook undisturbed for 5 minutes, until the bottom is slightly browned. Stir, then cook, stirring occasionally, until the cauliflower is tender, about 2 minutes.

4. Stir in the drained cranberries, kale, ¼ cup of the almonds, and the salt. Cover and cook until the kale is slightly tender and bright green, about 2 minutes. Add the vinegar and stir to combine. Transfer the mixture to a large bowl, cover, and keep warm.

5. To the skillet, add the green onions, remaining 1 tablespoon butter, and remaining ¼ cup almonds and cook, stirring occasionally, until the butter is melted, about 1 minute.

6. Serve the couscous warm, topped with the green onion/almond mixture.

Makes 8 servings

TIP: *If the couscous comes out a little dark, add 2 teaspoons of sherry to brighten it up.*

Vermicelli Salad

WITH PICKLED RED ONION

prep: *1 hour 20 minutes*   **cook:** *25 minutes*   **cool:** *none*

---

pickled red onion

2½ cups thinly sliced red onion (about 1 large)

¾ cup red wine vinegar

1½ tablespoons sugar

1 teaspoon kosher salt

dressing

⅓ cup rice vinegar

3 tablespoons honey

2 tablespoons fish sauce

1 garlic clove, minced

½ teaspoon grated fresh ginger (from a 1-inch piece)

½ teaspoon kosher salt

¼ teaspoon crushed red pepper flakes (optional)

¼ cup toasted sesame oil

vermicelli salad

8 ounces rice vermicelli

1½ cups grated carrots

1 cup cucumber matchsticks

3 tablespoons chopped fresh basil leaves

3 tablespoons chopped fresh cilantro leaves

3 tablespoons chopped fresh mint leaves

1 cup chopped salted roasted peanuts

1. To make the pickled red onion: Place the sliced onion in a heatproof container.

2. In a small saucepan, whisk together the vinegar, 1 cup water, the sugar, and salt. Bring to a boil over medium heat, whisking to dissolve the sugar, then let simmer for 5 minutes.

3. Remove the brine from the heat and carefully pour it over the onions. Let sit for at least 1 hour, then cover and refrigerate until ready to use.

4. Store in an airtight container in the refrigerator for up to 2 days.

5. To make the dressing: In a small skillet, whisk together the vinegar, honey, fish sauce, garlic, ginger, salt, and pepper flakes (if using). Bring to a simmer over medium heat and cook, whisking occasionally, until thickened and slightly reduced, 5 to 6 minutes. Remove from the heat and whisk in the sesame oil. Refrigerate until ready to use.

6. Meanwhile, to make the vermicelli salad: Cook the vermicelli according to the package directions. Strain the vermicelli in a colander and run cold water over it to cool the noodles. Drain well.

7. In a large bowl, toss the cooled noodles with the carrots, cucumber, pickled red onion, basil, cilantro, and mint. Pour the cooled dressing over the mixture and toss to coat.

8. Serve immediately or cover and store in the refrigerator until ready to serve. Top with the peanuts right before serving.

Makes 4 servings, with about 2 cups pickled red onion

Hasselback Potatoes

prep: *15 minutes*   **cook:** *1 hour 5 minutes*   **cool:** *none*

6 medium Yukon Gold
   potatoes

4 tablespoons (½ stick)
   unsalted butter, melted

2 tablespoons olive oil

1 teaspoon minced garlic

½ teaspoon sea salt

½ teaspoon freshly ground
   black pepper

3 tablespoons grated
   Parmesan cheese

2 tablespoons chopped fresh
   parsley

1. Preheat the oven to 425°F.

2. Using a knife, slice each potato crosswise into thin slices, taking care not to cut all the way through. (For even slicing, you can lay 2 wooden spoons or chopsticks along the sides of the potatoes as guides. This keeps the knife from cutting all the way through.)

3. Place the potatoes in a 9 × 13-inch or 7 × 11-inch baking dish and use your hands to carefully fan the potatoes out.

4. In a small bowl, whisk together the melted butter, olive oil, garlic, salt, and pepper.

5. Spoon the butter mixture over each potato, making sure to get in the cuts and coat the potatoes well, about 1 tablespoon per potato.

6. Bake, uncovered, for 45 minutes. Sprinkle the Parmesan and parsley evenly over each potato. Return to the oven and bake until the Parmesan is melted and a little crispy, about 20 minutes. Serve hot.

Makes 4 to 6 servings

Honey Thyme Roasted Carrots

prep: *15 minutes*   **cook:** *30 minutes*   **cool:** *none*

1 pound carrots, whole with tops on

3 tablespoons olive oil

1 tablespoon honey

1 tablespoon fresh lemon juice

½ teaspoon ground coriander

½ teaspoon ground cumin

2 teaspoons fresh thyme leaves

1 garlic clove, minced

½ teaspoon kosher salt

½ teaspoon freshly ground black pepper

1 tablespoon roughly chopped fresh parsley

1. Preheat the oven to 425°F. Line a sheet pan with foil.

2. Spread the carrots on the lined sheet pan.

3. In a small bowl, whisk together the oil, honey, lemon juice, coriander, cumin, thyme, garlic, salt, and pepper. Drizzle the mixture over the carrots, tossing to coat.

4. Roast until crisp-tender and golden, about 30 minutes, turning the carrots halfway through the cooking time.

5. Sprinkle with the parsley and serve hot.

Makes 4 servings

Roasted Rosemary Sweet Potatoes

prep: *10 minutes*   **cook:** *40 minutes*   **cool:** *none*

2 large sweet potatoes (8 to 10 ounces each), peeled and cut into ¼-inch strips

2 tablespoons olive oil

1 tablespoon minced fresh rosemary

2 teaspoons kosher salt

1 teaspoon freshly cracked black pepper

1. Preheat the oven to 450°F. Line a large sheet pan with foil.

2. In a large bowl, toss together the sweet potatoes, olive oil, rosemary, salt, and pepper. Spread out on the prepared sheet pan.

3. Roast until the sweet potatoes are browned and crispy, about 40 minutes, stirring occasionally. Serve warm.

Makes 4 to 6 servings

TIP: *Serve these sweet potatoes with Rib Eye Steaks (page 245).*

Cilantro Lime Rice

prep: *10 minutes*   **cook:** *under 25 minutes*   **cool:** *none*

4 tablespoons (½ stick) unsalted butter

1 cup basmati or long-grain white rice

1¾ cups chicken broth

½ teaspoon grated lime zest

2 tablespoons fresh lime juice

¼ cup chopped fresh cilantro

¼ teaspoon kosher salt

¼ teaspoon freshly ground black pepper

1. In a medium saucepan, melt 1 tablespoon of the butter over medium-high heat. Add the rice and sauté until the rice begins to brown a little, 2 to 3 minutes. Add the broth and bring to a boil over high heat. Reduce the heat to medium-low, cover, and simmer until tender, about 15 minutes. Fluff the rice with a fork.

2. Meanwhile, in a small glass bowl, melt the remaining 3 tablespoons butter in the microwave, about 30 seconds. Stir in the lime zest and juice.

3. Pour the lime butter over the hot rice, add the cilantro, and stir until combined. Season with the salt and pepper.

Makes 4 to 6 servings

TIP: *Cilantro Lime Rice goes well with Street Tacos (pages 247–249).*

Old-Fashioned Corn Casserole

prep: *10 minutes*   **cook:** *1 hour 5 minutes*   **cool:** *none*

Cooking spray

Two 15.25-ounce cans corn kernels, drained

One 14.75-ounce can cream-style corn

8 tablespoons (1 stick) unsalted butter, melted

12 ounces sharp Cheddar cheese, grated (about 3 cups)

One 8.5-ounce box Jiffy corn muffin mix

One 4-ounce can green chiles

2 large eggs

1 teaspoon kosher salt

½ teaspoon garlic powder

1½ teaspoons freshly ground black pepper

1. Preheat the oven to 350°F. Spray a 9 × 13-inch baking dish with cooking spray.

2. In a large bowl, combine the corn, creamed corn, melted butter, 2 cups of the Cheddar, the corn muffin mix, green chiles, eggs, salt, garlic powder, and pepper. Stir until well combined and pour evenly into the prepared baking dish.

3. Bake until set in the middle and the top is lightly golden, about 1 hour. Top with the remaining 1 cup Cheddar, return to the oven, and bake until the cheese is fully melted, about 5 minutes longer. Serve hot.

4. Store in an airtight container in the refrigerator for up to 5 days.

Makes 4 to 6 servings

Broccoli & Rice Casserole

prep: *20 minutes*   **cook:** *45 minutes*   **cool:** *none*

One 16-ounce package wild rice mix (about 2 cups uncooked)

4 cups (1 quart) chicken or vegetable broth

4 tablespoons (½ stick) unsalted butter

½ small yellow onion, cut into ¼-inch dice

3 garlic cloves, minced

1 tablespoon all-purpose flour

1 cup milk

Cooking spray

4 ounces cream cheese

8 ounces sharp Cheddar cheese, grated (about 2 cups)

1 teaspoon garlic salt

½ teaspoon kosher salt

1 teaspoon freshly ground black pepper

4 cups broccoli florets (from about 1 head), steamed until tender

1. In a medium saucepan, combine the wild rice mix and 3 cups of the chicken broth. Bring to a boil over medium heat, cover, reduce the heat to medium-low, and cook until the rice is tender and the broth is absorbed, about 30 minutes.

2. Meanwhile, in a large saucepan, melt the butter over medium heat. Add the onion and garlic and sauté until fragrant and slightly browned, about 3 minutes. Sprinkle in the flour and cook for 2 minutes to make a roux. Slowly stir in the milk and remaining 1 cup broth and stir until smooth and starting to thicken.

3. Preheat the oven to 350°F. Spray a 9 × 13-inch baking dish with cooking spray.

4. Add the cream cheese and 1 cup of the Cheddar to the roux and stir until the cheese is melted. Add the garlic salt, kosher salt, pepper, broccoli, and cooked wild rice and stir until well combined.

5. Pour the broccoli mixture into the prepared baking dish and top with the remaining 1 cup Cheddar. Bake until the cheese is melted and bubbling, 15 to 20 minutes. If you want a more browned top, broil the casserole for up to 5 minutes, watching it carefully.

6. Store in an airtight container in the refrigerator for up to 5 days.

Makes 6 servings

Onion Rings

WITH SPICY RANCH DRESSING

prep: *15 minutes*   **cook:** *25 minutes*   **cool:** *none*

spicy ranch dressing

1 cup mayonnaise, preferably
    Hellmann's

½ cup buttermilk

1 teaspoon garlic powder

1 teaspoon onion powder

½ teaspoon table salt

½ teaspoon freshly ground
    black pepper

⅓ teaspoon cayenne pepper

½ teaspoon dried dill

½ teaspoon paprika

onion rings

Vegetable oil, for deep-frying

1¼ cups all-purpose flour

¼ cup sugar

1 teaspoon kosher salt, plus
    more for sprinkling

¾ teaspoon baking powder

1 large egg

1 cup whole milk

1 large yellow onion, cut into
    ½-inch-thick slices and
    separated into rings

1. To make the spicy ranch dressing: In a 1-pint screw-top jar, combine the mayonnaise, buttermilk, garlic powder, onion powder, salt, black pepper, cayenne, dill, and paprika. Screw on the lid and shake well. Reserve the dressing in the refrigerator. Store the remaining dressing in the refrigerator for 4 to 5 days.

2. Preheat the oven to 350°F.

3. To make the onion rings: Pour 3 inches of the oil into a large Dutch oven. Set a wire rack on a sheet pan and have it at the ready. Heat the oil to 375°F on a deep-fry thermometer.

4. In a medium bowl, combine the flour, sugar, salt, and the baking powder. Add the egg and milk and whisk until the batter is smooth.

5. Dip the onion rings into the batter and let any excess drip off. Working in batches of 5 or 6, place the onions in the hot oil and fry until deep golden brown, turning halfway through, about 3 minutes total.

6. Transfer the onion rings to the wire rack as they are fried and sprinkle with kosher salt. Place in the oven to keep warm.

7. Serve hot with the spicy ranch dressing.

Makes 6 servings, with 1½ cups dressing

Overnight Black-Eyed Peas

prep: *10 minutes, plus 8 hours soaking*   **cook:** *3 hours 25 minutes*   **cool:** *none*

2 pounds dried black-eyed
peas

3 tablespoons unsalted butter

½ pound pork shoulder

1¼ cups small-diced yellow
onion (about 1 large)

6 garlic cloves, minced

¼ teaspoon cayenne pepper

1 teaspoon paprika

6 cups (1½ quarts) chicken
broth

One 14.5-ounce can stewed
tomatoes, drained

One 4-ounce can diced green
chiles

4 bay leaves

1 tablespoon kosher salt

¼ cup apple cider vinegar

1. In a large bowl, combine the peas with water to cover by 3 inches. Soak for 8 hours or overnight. Drain the peas and set them aside.

2. In a large soup pot, melt the butter over medium-high heat. Add the pork and sear until golden brown all over, 3 to 4 minutes per side. Add the onion, garlic, cayenne, and paprika and cook, stirring frequently, until the onion is tender, 3 to 4 minutes.

3. Add the broth, drained black-eyed peas, the stewed tomatoes, chiles, and bay leaves. Bring to a boil, then reduce the heat to medium-low, cover, and simmer, stirring occasionally, until the peas are tender, about 3 hours.

4. Discard the bay leaves, stir in the salt and vinegar, and serve hot.

5. Store in an airtight container in the refrigerator for 3 to 5 days. Add a little chicken broth before reheating.

Makes 8 servings

TIP: *These black-eyed peas are terrific served with cornbread and are a good choice to take to a potluck.*

Potato Salad

prep: *30 minutes, plus 10 minutes chilling*   **cook:** *15 minutes*   **cool:** *2 hours*

¾ teaspoon kosher salt

1¼ pounds red potatoes

6 large eggs

1¼ cups mayonnaise,
preferably Hellmann's

3 tablespoons yellow mustard

1½ tablespoons apple cider
vinegar

¾ teaspoon garlic powder

¾ teaspoon freshly ground
black pepper

½ cup small-diced celery
(about 1 stalk)

½ cup sliced green onions

¼ teaspoon paprika, for
garnish

1. Bring a large pot of lightly salted water to a boil. Add the potatoes and cook until tender but still firm, about 15 minutes. Drain, cool, and cut into ¾- to 1-inch chunks.

2. Meanwhile, set up a bowl of ice and water. In a medium saucepan, cover the eggs with cold water. Bring to a boil over medium heat, cover, remove from the heat, and let the eggs stand in the hot water for 12 minutes. Transfer the eggs to the ice water and let them chill for 10 minutes. Peel the eggs and cut them into 1-inch chunks.

3. In a medium bowl, stir together the mayonnaise, mustard, vinegar, garlic powder, ¼ teaspoon salt, and the pepper until well combined. In a large bowl, combine the potatoes, eggs, celery, and green onions. Pour over the dressing and mix well. Refrigerate until chilled, about 2 hours.

4. Sprinkle with the paprika and serve.

5. Store in an airtight container in the refrigerator for up to 5 days.

Makes 10 servings

TIP: *This potato salad is a great gathering option and works as a nice side with Brisket Sliders (page 263).*

Zucchini Squash Strata

prep: *1 hour 15 minutes, plus 1 hour chilling*   **cook:** *55 minutes*   **cool:** *none*

I could eat this vegetable strata every week and never tire of it. The layer of bread at the bottom of the dish soaks up the cheese blend while it bakes, so that each slice is full of many delicious flavors. I like to bring this to a weekend brunch or potluck because it's one of those unexpected dishes that inevitably ends up being devoured well before any of the usual favorites.

7 cups torn French bread (from 2 large loaves)

2 tablespoons olive oil

3 tablespoons unsalted butter, plus more for the baking dish

4 large zucchini, cut into ⅛-inch-thick slices

4 large yellow squash, cut into ⅛-inch-thick slices

6 ounces white Cheddar cheese, grated (about 1½ cups)

4 ounces Fontina cheese, shredded (about 1 cup)

2 ounces Parmesan cheese, grated (about ½ cup)

2 teaspoons garlic salt

8 large eggs

1½ cups whole milk

½ teaspoon kosher salt

½ teaspoon freshly ground black pepper

3 tablespoons roughly chopped fresh parsley

1. Preheat the oven to 250°F.

2. Spread the torn bread on a sheet pan and dry in the oven for 45 minutes until crunchy and golden brown. Set aside.

3. In a large skillet, heat the oil and butter over medium heat. Add the zucchini and squash and sauté until golden brown, 15 to 18 minutes. Transfer to a plate or bowl to cool completely, 20 to 30 minutes.

4. Grease a 9 × 13-inch baking dish with butter.

5. In a large bowl, mix the bread, Cheddar, Fontina, Parmesan, sautéed zucchini/squash mixture, and garlic salt until combined.

6. In a separate large bowl, whisk together the eggs, milk, salt, and pepper until smooth.

7. Pour the egg mixture over the zucchini and bread mixture and stir until the bread is well coated. Spoon the mixture into the prepared baking dish. Cover the dish tightly with plastic wrap and refrigerate for at least 1 hour or up to overnight.

8. Preheat the oven to 350°F.

9. Remove the plastic wrap and bake the strata until the casserole is set and the top is nicely browned, 35 to 40 minutes.

10. Sprinkle with the parsley and serve hot.

11. Store in an airtight container in the refrigerator for up to 3 days.

Makes 8 to 10 servings

Spring Vegetable Risotto

prep: *40 minutes*   **cook:** *1 hour*   **cool:** *none*

5 cups chicken broth

8 tablespoons (1 stick) unsalted butter

1 leek (white part only), thinly sliced

16 ounces assorted mushrooms, such as button, shiitake, or portobello, sliced

2 teaspoons kosher salt

1½ teaspoons freshly ground black pepper

2 garlic cloves, minced

2 cups Arborio rice

½ cup dry white wine

1 cup trimmed and quartered radishes

2 ounces Parmesan cheese, grated (about ½ cup)

¼ cup heavy cream

1 tablespoon grated lemon zest

2 tablespoons fresh lemon juice

1 cup frozen peas, thawed

2 cups fresh spinach

1 teaspoon fresh thyme leaves

2 tablespoons minced chives

1. In a medium saucepan, bring the chicken broth to a simmer over medium-high heat. Reduce the heat to low and set aside to keep warm.

2. In a large soup pot or Dutch oven, melt 3 tablespoons of the butter over medium-high heat. Add the leek and mushrooms and sprinkle with the salt and pepper. Sauté, stirring occasionally, until the mushrooms are golden brown and the leeks are soft, 8 to 10 minutes. Add the garlic and stir until softened and fragrant, about 1 minute.

3. Add the rice and stir constantly until the rice begins to turn translucent and starts to develop a nutty scent, 2 to 3 minutes. Add the wine and stir until the rice has soaked up all the liquid and any browned bits on the bottom of the pan have been released. Reduce the heat to medium. Carefully ladle 1 cup of the warm chicken broth into the rice mixture, stirring constantly until the rice soaks up all the liquid. Repeat by adding 1 cup of broth at a time and stirring until absorbed. The risotto will thicken as the starch is released.

4. Meanwhile, in a small skillet, melt 3 tablespoons of the butter over medium heat and add the radishes. Cook, stirring occasionally, until the edges are golden brown, 4 to 5 minutes. Remove from the heat.

5. When all the liquid has been absorbed into the rice mixture and it is creamy and thick, add the Parmesan, cream, ½ tablespoon of the lemon zest, the lemon juice, peas, and spinach. Stir to combine until the spinach is wilted. Add the thyme, 1 tablespoon of the chives, the radishes, and the remaining 2 tablespoons butter, stirring until the butter is melted and absorbed.

6. Garnish with the remaining 1 tablespoon chives and ½ tablespoon lemon zest. Serve warm as a main dish or as a side.

7. Store in an airtight container in the refrigerator for up to 1 day. Reheat in the microwave.

Makes 6 servings

Greek Pasta Salad

prep: *20 minutes*   **cook:** *15 minutes*   **cool:** *1 hour*

1 pound bow tie (farfalle) pasta

⅓ cup rice vinegar

¼ cup olive oil

2 garlic cloves, minced

1 teaspoon kosher salt

1 teaspoon freshly ground black pepper

¾ cup pitted halved kalamata olives

½ cup chopped green onions

½ cup chopped fresh basil leaves

1 cup drained stewed whole tomatoes (from one 15-ounce can), roughly chopped

4 ounces feta cheese, crumbled (about 1 cup)

1. Cook the pasta according to the package directions and drain.

2. Meanwhile, in a medium bowl, whisk together the vinegar, oil, garlic, salt, and pepper.

3. Place the drained pasta in a large bowl and pour the dressing on top. Add the olives, green onions, basil, and stewed tomatoes and toss well. Add the feta and toss again.

4. Chill for 1 hour before serving.

5. Store in an airtight container in the refrigerator for 2 to 4 days.

Makes 6 servings

Macaroni Salad

prep: *15 minutes*　　**cook:** *20 minutes*　　**cool:** *15 minutes*

8 ounces elbow macaroni

1½ cups mayonnaise, preferably Hellmann's

1 tablespoon champagne vinegar or apple cider vinegar

1 tablespoon Dijon mustard

1 teaspoon sugar

1 teaspoon kosher salt

½ teaspoon ground white pepper

2 celery stalks, cut into small dice

1 cup diced red bell pepper (about 1 medium)

¼ cup diced red onion

¼ cup chopped fresh parsley

1. Cook the macaroni according to the package directions. Drain and let cool for 15 minutes.

2. In a large bowl, whisk together the mayonnaise, vinegar, mustard, sugar, salt, and white pepper until well combined.

3. Add the drained and cooled macaroni, the celery, bell pepper, onion, and parsley. Toss to coat evenly.

4. Refrigerate for at least 15 minutes to allow the flavors to meld. Serve chilled or at room temperature.

5. Store in an airtight container in the refrigerator for up to 3 days.

Makes 10 servings

Creamy Polenta

prep: *5 minutes*   **cook:** *20 minutes*   **cool:** *none*

4 cups (1 quart) water or chicken broth

1 teaspoon kosher salt

1 cup polenta or yellow cornmeal

4 tablespoons (½ stick) unsalted butter, cut into pieces

3 ounces Parmesan cheese, grated (about ¾ cup)

1. In a medium saucepan, bring the water and salt to a boil over high heat.

2. Slowly whisk in the polenta until well combined. Reduce the heat to medium-low and cook, whisking constantly, until thick and creamy, 10 to 15 minutes.

3. Add the butter and Parmesan and stir until smooth and creamy. Serve warm.

Makes 6 servings

polenta squares

For an alternative use, pour the finished polenta onto a small sheet pan and spread it out evenly with a spatula. Refrigerate for 20 minutes until cool. Cut the polenta into squares. In a nonstick skillet, melt 1 tablespoon butter over medium heat. Add the polenta squares and cook until golden brown on both sides, about 2 minutes per side. Serve immediately or cover tightly with plastic wrap and store overnight in the refrigerator.

TIP: *This polenta is delicious with Rib Eye Steaks (page 245).*

Bulgur Salad

prep: *20 minutes*   **cook:** *under 25 minutes*   **cool:** *1 hour*

1½ cups (9.75 ounces) bulgur, regular or light (golden)

2 teaspoons kosher salt, plus more to taste

2 cups boiling water

4 tablespoons good-quality extra virgin olive oil

⅓ cup diced green onion

¾ cup diced red bell pepper

1½ cups medium-diced English cucumber

¼ cup finely chopped fresh dill, plus sprigs for garnish

⅓ cup finely chopped fresh parsley

One 15-ounce can chickpeas, rinsed well and drained

6 tablespoons fresh lemon juice (from about 2 large), plus more to taste

1 garlic clove, finely minced

½ teaspoon freshly ground black pepper, plus more to taste

Freshly cracked black pepper and flaky sea salt, such as Maldon

1. Place the bulgur in a large heatproof bowl with 1 teaspoon of the kosher salt and the boiling water. Cover the bowl tightly with plastic wrap and let sit until all the water is absorbed, 20 to 25 minutes.

2. Add the remaining 1 teaspoon kosher salt, 3 tablespoons of the olive oil, the green onion, bell pepper, cucumber, dill, parsley, chickpeas, lemon juice, garlic, and ground black pepper. Stir, taste for seasonings, and add more salt, pepper, or lemon juice, if desired.

3. Top with dill sprigs, cracked black pepper, and flaky sea salt. Drizzle with the remaining 1 tablespoon olive oil. Chill for at least 1 hour before serving.

4. Store in an airtight container in the refrigerator for up to 3 days.

Makes 6 servings

Homemade Green Bean Casserole

prep: *15 minutes*   **cook:** *1 hour*   **cool:** *none*

1 large yellow onion, thinly sliced

⅓ cup cornstarch

1 teaspoon seasoned salt

Canola oil, for deep-frying

5 tablespoons unsalted butter, melted

¼ cup panko bread crumbs

1 tablespoon plus 1 teaspoon kosher salt

2 pounds green beans, ends snapped

Two 8-ounce packages sliced mushrooms

1 teaspoon freshly ground black pepper

2 garlic cloves, minced

¼ teaspoon ground nutmeg

⅓ cup all-purpose flour

¾ cup chicken broth

1¾ cups heavy cream

1. Preheat the oven to 375°F. Lightly grease a 9 × 11-inch baking dish.

2. In a large bowl, combine the onion slices, cornstarch, and seasoned salt and toss until the onions are well coated.

3. Pour 3 inches of oil into a deep medium saucepan. Have ready a wire rack lined with paper towels to use for draining. Heat the oil to 350°F on a deep-fry thermometer.

4. Working in batches, use a slotted spoon to lower half the onions into the hot oil. Cook, stirring occasionally, until golden, 2 to 3 minutes. Use a slotted spoon to remove the onions to the paper towel–lined rack. Repeat to fry the remaining onions. Set aside.

5. In a small bowl, mix 1 tablespoon of the butter and the panko. Set aside.

6. Set up a large bowl of ice and water. Bring a large pot of water with 1 tablespoon of the salt to a boil over medium-high heat. Add the green beans and cook until crisp-tender, about 6 minutes. Using tongs, carefully remove the green beans to the ice water to stop the cooking process. Cool in the ice water for 1 to 2 minutes, then drain the beans. Set aside.

7. In a large skillet, heat the remaining 4 tablespoons butter over medium-high heat. Add the mushrooms and cook, stirring frequently, until golden brown, 2 to 3 minutes. Add the remaining 1 teaspoon salt, the pepper, garlic, and nutmeg and stir to combine.

8. Sprinkle the flour over the mushrooms and stir to combine well. Slowly whisk in the chicken broth, bring to a simmer, and cook until well incorporated, about 2 minutes. Reduce the heat to medium and slowly whisk in the cream, stirring until the sauce thickens, 4 to 6 minutes. Remove from the heat and stir in the green beans. Pour into the prepared baking dish and top with the buttered panko.

9. Transfer to the oven and bake until bubbling, 15 to 20 minutes. Top with the fried onions and serve.

10. Store in an airtight container in the refrigerator for up to 2 days.

Makes 6 to 8 servings

Southern Sweet Potato Casserole

prep: *20 minutes, plus 20 minutes chilling*   **cook:** *1 hour 40 minutes*   **cool:** *none*

sweet potatoes

5 pounds sweet potatoes

Cooking spray

1 cup sugar

½ cup heavy cream

8 tablespoons (1 stick) unsalted butter, at room temperature

⅓ cup whole milk

2 large eggs

1½ teaspoon pure vanilla extract

¾ teaspoon kosher salt

topping

1 cup cornflakes, crushed

⅓ cup chopped pecans

3 tablespoons light brown sugar

4 tablespoons (½ stick) unsalted butter, melted

2 cups mini marshmallows

1. Preheat the oven to 450°F.

2. For the sweet potatoes: Poke each sweet potato a few times with a fork, wrap them individually in foil, and roast until tender, about 1 hour 15 minutes. Remove from the oven to cool, about 20 minutes. Leave the oven on, but reduce the temperature to 375°F.

3. Spray a 9 × 13-inch baking dish with cooking spray.

4. When the sweet potatoes are cool enough to handle, peel them and place in a large bowl. Break up the potatoes slightly with a fork. Add the sugar, cream, butter, milk, eggs, vanilla, and salt. Using a handheld mixer, whip the potato mixture until well combined, 3 to 5 minutes.

5. Scrape the mixture into the prepared baking dish and spread it out evenly.

6. For the topping: In a medium bowl, mix together the cornflakes, pecans, brown sugar, and melted butter. Sprinkle the mixture evenly over the sweet potatoes and bake until golden brown, about 20 minutes. Turn the oven to broil and position an oven rack 4 to 5 inches from the broiler element.

7. Sprinkle the marshmallows on top of the casserole and broil until the marshmallows begin to brown and bubble, about 1 minute, watching carefully. Serve hot.

8. Store in an airtight container in the refrigerator for up to 3 days. Reheat in a 350°F oven for 10 minutes or in a microwave for 3 to 5 minutes.

Makes 10 to 12 servings

CHAPTER SEVEN

Dinner

DINNER GATHERS US AT
DAY'S END, WHEN STORIES ARE
TOLD, MEMORIES ARE FORMED,
AND TRADITIONS ARE MADE

Whole Roasted Chicken

WITH ROASTED POTATOES, CARROTS, AND BROCCOLINI

prep: *15 minutes*   **cook:** *1 hour 25 minutes*   **cool:** *15 minutes*

One 4-pound whole chicken

1 tablespoon olive oil

1½ teaspoons kosher salt

¾ teaspoon coarsely ground black pepper

1½ pounds baby potato medley or tricolored baby potatoes

6 large tricolored carrots, trimmed and cut into thirds, or 4 cups tricolored baby carrots

1 medium yellow onion, quartered

4 tablespoons (½ stick) unsalted butter

¼ cup good-quality dry white wine

2 garlic cloves, chopped

Grated zest of 1 lemon

1 tablespoon fresh lemon juice

1 teaspoon garlic salt

1 bunch broccolini or 1 broccoli head, cut into 1-inch florets

1 tablespoon minced fresh parsley

1. Preheat the oven to 425°F.

2. Tie the legs of the chicken together with kitchen string. Place the chicken in the center of a sheet pan. Rub the skin with the oil and sprinkle evenly with the salt and pepper. Arrange the potatoes, carrots, and onion quarters around the chicken.

3. In a small saucepan, melt the butter over medium heat. Stir in the wine, garlic, lemon zest, lemon juice, and garlic salt and cook for 1 minute. Drizzle half the wine sauce over the vegetables, tossing to coat.

4. Bake for 35 minutes. Reduce the oven temperature to 325°F, add the broccolini to the pan, and bake until an instant-read thermometer inserted into a thick thigh registers 165°F, 40 to 45 minutes. Baste the chicken with the remaining wine sauce in the last 10 minutes of cooking.

5. Remove the pan from the oven, tent the chicken and vegetables with foil, and let it sit for 15 minutes. Cut the chicken into slices to serve, or serve family style, cutting the chicken into 8 pieces.

6. Sprinkle the vegetables with the parsley.

Makes 4 servings

TIP: *Serve the chicken and vegetables with a petite salad.*

Orecchiette Pancetta

prep: *20 minutes*   **cook:** *30 minutes*   **cool:** *none*

1 pound orecchiette pasta

3 tablespoons unsalted butter

4 ounces pancetta or bacon, diced

1 medium shallot, thinly sliced

1 garlic clove, minced

1 cup chicken broth

¾ cup heavy cream

8 ounces Parmesan cheese, grated (about 2 cups), plus more for garnish

1 cup frozen peas, thawed

2 tablespoons fresh lemon juice

1 tablespoon minced chives

2½ teaspoons kosher salt

½ teaspoon freshly ground black pepper

Freshly cracked black pepper

1. Cook the pasta according to the package directions. Drain and set aside.

2. Meanwhile, in a large skillet, heat 1 tablespoon of the butter over medium heat. Add the pancetta and cook, stirring occasionally, until crispy, about 4 minutes. Add the shallot, reduce the heat to medium-low, and sauté until translucent, about 6 minutes. Add the garlic and sauté until fragrant, about 1 minute.

3. Drain the grease from the pan and remove the pancetta mixture to a bowl.

4. Melt the remaining 2 tablespoons butter in the pan over medium-high heat until it starts to bubble. Whisk in the chicken broth and cream and bring to a simmer, then reduce the heat to medium low. Add the Parmesan and whisk until melted. Add the pancetta mixture, peas, lemon juice, chives, salt, and ground black pepper. Whisk until the sauce begins to thicken, about 3 minutes.

5. Add the drained pasta to the pan and toss to coat.

6. Serve garnished with Parmesan and cracked black pepper.

Makes 6 servings

Philly Cheesesteaks

prep: *35 minutes, plus 10 minutes chilling*   **cook:** *under 35 minutes*   **cool:** *none*

2 pounds rib eye or strip steak

3 tablespoons olive oil

2 teaspoons fajita seasoning

1 tablespoon unsalted butter

1 medium yellow onion, sliced
   into thick rounds

½ teaspoon kosher salt

½ teaspoon freshly ground
   black pepper

1 large yellow bell pepper, cut
   into ½-inch-wide strips

1 large red bell pepper, cut
   into ½-inch-wide strips

2 poblano peppers, seeded
   and cut into ½-inch-wide
   strips

6 hoagie or steak rolls, split
   but not sliced all the way
   through

12 slices pepper Jack or
   provolone cheese

1. Freeze the steaks for 10 minutes to make them easier to slice. Remove the steaks from the freezer and slice against the grain into long, ¼-inch-wide strips.

2. In a large skillet, heat 1 tablespoon of the oil over high heat. Add half the sliced steak, season with ½ teaspoon of the fajita seasoning, and sear, stirring occasionally, until browned, 3 to 4 minutes. Transfer the steak to a plate and cover with foil. Repeat with 1 tablespoon of the oil, the remaining steak, and ½ teaspoon of the fajita seasoning. Reserve with the rest of the steak.

3. Reduce the heat under the skillet to medium-high. Add the butter and remaining 1 tablespoon oil and heat until the butter bubbles. Add the onion, salt, and black pepper and sauté until the onion is softened and translucent, 4 to 5 minutes.

4. Add the bell peppers, poblano peppers, and the remaining 1 teaspoon fajita seasoning and sauté, stirring often, until the onions and peppers are caramelized, 15 to 20 minutes.

5. Position a rack 4 to 5 inches from the heat and turn the broiler to high. Line a sheet pan with foil.

6. Add the steak to the skillet, toss to combine, and heat through, about 5 minutes. Remove from the heat.

7. Open the rolls and set them on the lined sheet pan. Using tongs, divide the steak and pepper mixture among the rolls and cover the steak with 2 slices of cheese per open-faced sandwich.

8. Broil the sandwiches until the cheese begins to bubble, 2 to 3 minutes.

Makes 6 servings

Chicken Pecan Asparagus Casserole

prep: *25 minutes* **cook:** *1 hour 5 minutes* **cool:** *30 minutes*

Cooking spray

1 teaspoon olive oil

1½ cups small-diced yellow onion (about 1 large)

2 cups finely chopped toasted pecans

¾ cup all-purpose flour

5 tablespoons unsalted butter, melted

1 cup sour cream

½ cup heavy cream

1 teaspoon dried dill

1 teaspoon kosher salt

½ teaspoon freshly ground black pepper

6 large eggs

2 cups shredded cooked chicken breast (home-roasted or rotisserie chicken)

1 pound asparagus, ends trimmed

8 ounces Cheddar cheese, grated (about 2 cups)

1. Preheat the oven to 350°F. Spray a 9 × 13-inch baking dish with cooking spray.

2. Heat a small skillet over medium-high heat. Add the oil and swirl to coat. Add the onion and sauté until tender, 4 to 5 minutes. Set aside to cool.

3. In a food processor, pulse the pecans and flour until the pecans are finely chopped. Transfer to a bowl and stir in the melted butter until a dough forms.

4. Press the dough evenly into the bottom of the baking dish. Bake until browned and toasted, 25 to 28 minutes. Set aside to cool for at least 5 minutes. Leave the oven on.

5. In a large bowl, whisk together the sour cream, heavy cream, dill, salt, pepper, and eggs. Stir in the sautéed onion and shredded chicken and pour evenly over the crust mixture. With a long side of the baking dish facing you, start at the left short side and lay the asparagus evenly across the width of the chicken mixture and parallel to one another. Sprinkle evenly with the Cheddar.

6. Bake until the cheese is slightly browned and bubbling on the edges, about 35 minutes. Let cool for at least 30 minutes before serving. Cut into squares.

7. Store in an airtight container in the refrigerator for up to 3 days.

Makes 8 servings

Sunday Pot Roast

prep: *15 minutes*   **cook:** *4 hours 25 minutes*   **cool:** *none*

I'll always be grateful for a dinner that's prepared by simply tossing a bunch of ingredients into a pot, walking away for a few hours, and returning to a delicious home-cooked meal—with very little cleanup. But this particular recipe has earned its name because of what it's come to symbolize for our family. Sundays in our house are for rest, and to reset. A simmering pot roast is a subtle reminder to our family to take it easy. So, a few years ago, I dubbed this recipe the Sunday Pot Roast. It sits and simmers and cooks hour by hour, and by the end of the day, it gathers all of us around the dinner table. But, of course, there's no wrong day of the week to make a really good, really simple pot roast.

One 5-pound chuck (pot) roast

3 tablespoons olive oil

1 tablespoon kosher salt

1 tablespoon freshly ground black pepper

4 large russet potatoes, peeled and cut into 2-inch chunks

8 large carrots, cut into 2- to 3-inch chunks

1 white onion, halved

2 garlic cloves, smashed

2 cups beef broth

¼ cup Worcestershire

4 thyme sprigs

1. Preheat the oven to 300°F.

2. Rub the roast with the olive oil and sprinkle it evenly with the salt and pepper.

3. In a large Dutch oven over medium-high heat, sear the roast until browned on all sides, 6 to 8 minutes per side.

4. Add the potatoes, carrots, onion, garlic, beef broth, Worcestershire, and thyme to the pot. Cover, transfer to the oven, and roast until the meat falls apart and the vegetables are fork tender, about 4 hours.

5. Serve the pot roast hot with the vegetables.

6. Store in an airtight container in the refrigerator for up to 3 days.

Makes 6 servings

TIP: *The leftovers make a nice sandwich.*

Shrimp & Grits

prep: *10 minutes*   **cook:** *under 25 minutes*   **cool:** *none*

2 cups chicken broth

1 cup quick-cooking grits

1 teaspoon kosher salt

8 ounces sharp white
Cheddar cheese, grated
(about 2 cups)

½ cup heavy cream

3 tablespoons unsalted butter

1 teaspoon garlic powder

Freshly ground black pepper

4 slices thick-cut bacon,
chopped

1 pound large shrimp, peeled
and deveined

1 garlic clove, minced

1 tablespoon minced chives

1 teaspoon smoked paprika

1. In a large saucepan, combine the broth and 2½ cups water and bring to a boil over high heat. Pour in the grits and salt, stirring constantly. Reduce the heat to low and simmer, stirring occasionally, until the grits thicken, about 8 minutes. Stir in the Cheddar, cream, butter, garlic powder, and pepper. Remove from the heat and cover to keep warm.

2. In a skillet, cook the bacon over medium heat, stirring occasionally, until crispy, about 8 minutes. Use a slotted spoon to remove the bacon to paper towels, reserving the drippings in the pan.

3. Increase the heat to medium-high and add the shrimp and garlic to the skillet. Cook, stirring occasionally, until the shrimp turn pink, 4 to 6 minutes.

4. Divide the grits among four bowls and top with the shrimp and bacon and a sprinkling of chives and paprika.

5. Store in an airtight container in the refrigerator for 3 to 5 days.

Makes 4 servings

Chicken Piccata

WITH ROASTED ZUCCHINI AND MEYER LEMONS

prep: *20 minutes, plus 2 hours chilling*   **cook:** *under 25 minutes*   **cool:** *none*

4 boneless, skinless chicken breasts (about 6 to 8 ounces each)

3 Meyer lemons

3 garlic cloves, minced

4 tablespoons olive oil

2 cups panko bread crumbs

3 medium zucchini, cut into 1½-inch cubes

1 teaspoon kosher salt

1 teaspoon freshly ground black pepper

2 tablespoons drained capers

4 ounces Parmesan cheese, freshly grated (about 1 cup)

1 tablespoon chopped fresh parsley

1. Position racks in the top and bottom thirds of the oven and preheat the oven to 375°F.

2. Place the chicken breasts between two sheets of plastic wrap and use a meat pounder or heavy skillet to pound them to less than a 1-inch thickness. Cut the chicken into 3-inch-long strips and place them in a large bowl.

3. Squeeze the juice of 2 of the lemons into the bowl and add the garlic and 3 tablespoons of the olive oil. Toss to coat well. Cover the bowl and marinate the chicken in the refrigerator for at least 2 hours.

4. When ready to cook, place the panko in a shallow dish. Press the chicken strips into the panko to coat them evenly, then place them on a sheet pan. (Discard the marinade.)

5. On another sheet pan, toss the zucchini with the remaining 1 tablespoon olive oil.

6. Sprinkle the chicken and zucchini evenly with the salt and pepper. Cut the remaining lemon in half and place one half, cut side up, on each pan.

7. Place the chicken pan on the top oven rack and the zucchini pan on the bottom oven rack. Bake for 18 minutes. Remove the zucchini and transfer to a serving bowl.

8. Turn the oven to broil and broil the chicken until golden brown, about 5 minutes.

9. Sprinkle the capers over the chicken, then sprinkle with Parmesan. Squeeze the baked lemons on top of the chicken and zucchini. Sprinkle with parsley and serve.

Makes 4 servings

Chicken Mushroom Spinach Crêpes

WITH MUSHROOM SAUCE

prep: *25 minutes*   **cook:** *40 minutes*   **cool:** *none*

crêpes

1 cup all-purpose flour

2 large eggs

¾ cup whole milk

2 tablespoons unsalted butter, melted

½ teaspoon kosher salt

1 teaspoon chopped fresh dill (optional), plus more for garnish

Cooking spray

filling and sauce

3 tablespoons unsalted butter

1 pound sliced baby bella mushrooms

2 garlic cloves, minced

2 cups heavy cream

1½ teaspoons garlic salt

¾ teaspoon ground white pepper

4 ounces Parmesan cheese, grated (about 1 cup)

2 cups baby spinach

2 cups shredded cooked chicken breast (home-roasted or rotisserie chicken)

1. To make the crêpes: In a blender, combine the flour, eggs, milk, ½ cup water, melted butter, and salt. Blend until completely smooth, scraping down the sides as needed, about 1 minute.

2. Pour into a large liquid measuring cup and add the dill (if using), stirring to combine.

3. Heat a 10-inch nonstick skillet over medium heat and spray with cooking spray. Add ¼ cup batter and tilt the pan to make sure the mixture evenly and lightly coats the skillet. Cook 1 to 2 minutes, until the crêpe is lightly browned. Flip to cook the other side, about 1 minute.

4. Set the crêpes aside to roll with filling or fold them into quarters and top with sauce. The crêpes can be made ahead up to 2 hours, covered, and refrigerated.

5. To make the filling and sauce: In a large skillet, heat the butter over medium-high heat. Add the mushrooms and cook in one layer, without disturbing, until browned, about 4 minutes. Flip and continue cooking until tender and browned, stirring occasionally, about 5 minutes.

6. Add the garlic and stir constantly until fragrant, about 1 minute. Stir in the cream, garlic salt, and white pepper and simmer, stirring occasionally to check the consistency, until thickened, 5 to 8 minutes. Add the Parmesan and stir until smooth and melted.

7. Measure out ¾ cup of the mushroom sauce and set aside in a small bowl. Add the spinach to the sauce remaining in the pan and cook, stirring often, until the spinach is wilted, approximately 2 minutes.

8. Fold in the chicken and cook until heated through, about 1 minute.

9. If filling the crêpes, spoon ¼ cup chicken mixture onto each crêpe and roll up. Serve filled or folded crêpes immediately, topped with reserved mushroom sauce and dill.

Makes 8 crêpes

Italian Chicken Stack

prep: *15 minutes*   **cook:** *25 minutes*   **cool:** *none*

Canola oil, for deep-frying,
    plus 2 tablespoons

4 boneless, skinless chicken
    breasts (about 6 to
    8 ounces each)

¾ cup all-purpose flour

½ teaspoon plus ⅛ teaspoon
    kosher salt

¼ teaspoon freshly ground
    black pepper

4 tablespoons (½ stick)
    unsalted butter

1 cup chicken broth

1 pound asparagus, ends
    trimmed

1 tablespoon cornstarch

4 thin slices ham (about
    1 ounce each)

8 large fresh basil leaves

4 thin slices Fontina cheese

2 teaspoons balsamic glaze

1. Pour 1 inch of canola oil into a large saucepan over medium-high heat. Have ready a wire rack lined with paper towels to use for draining. Heat the oil to 350°F on a deep-fry thermometer and keep hot until ready to fry.

2. Meanwhile, place the chicken breasts between two sheets of plastic wrap and use a meat pounder or heavy skillet to gently pound them to a 1-inch thickness.

3. In a shallow dish, combine the flour, ½ teaspoon of the salt, and the pepper and stir to combine. Using a paper towel, pat the chicken dry and dredge in the flour mixture, shaking to remove any excess.

4. In a large skillet, heat 2 tablespoons of the butter and the 2 tablespoons canola oil over medium-high heat. Brown the chicken breasts on both sides, 5 to 6 minutes per side. Be careful not to crowd the pan; you may need to work in batches. Transfer the chicken to a platter and set aside, covered, with a foil tent to keep warm.

5. Add the chicken broth to the skillet, bring to a simmer, and cook for 2 to 3 minutes, whisking constantly to get all the browned bits from the bottom of the pan. Add the remaining 2 tablespoons butter, still whisking constantly.

6. Return the chicken to the pan and reduce the heat to low. Using a spoon, drizzle the pan sauce over the chicken and cook until the sauce has thickened, 4 to 5 minutes. Keep covered in foil or in a warm oven.

7. Use a vegetable peeler to cut the asparagus into ribbons to equal about 2 packed cups. Combine with the cornstarch in a large bowl and toss to coat.

8. Working in batches, fry the asparagus ribbons in the oil, tossing with a slotted spoon or spider occasionally, until crispy and starting to turn golden brown, 10 to 15 seconds. Remove to the paper towel–lined rack and sprinkle immediately with the remaining ⅛ teaspoon salt. Set aside.

9. To assemble, lay 1 slice of ham, 2 basil leaves, and 1 slice of Fontina on each chicken breast. Cook over medium heat for 2 to 3 minutes, using a spoon to drizzle the sauce on top to baste the chicken and melt the cheese.

10. Plate the chicken breasts, top each with a mound of asparagus ribbons, and drizzle each with ½ teaspoon balsamic glaze. Serve immediately, with the leftover sauce on the side.

Makes 4 servings

Cacio e Pepe

prep: *10 minutes*   **cook:** *20 minutes*   **cool:** *none*

I found out that I was pregnant with Crew shortly before Chip and I took a trip to Italy with a few of our dear friends. Most of the restaurants we dined in served these incredibly rich, decadent Italian dishes. Normally, I would be all-in for that kind of meal, but my first trimester had me craving simplicity. So, anywhere we ate, I would ask the waiter if the kitchen could make me a simple plate of cacio e pepe. While its name might sound like it's going to be a complicated dish, it basically translates to "cheese and pepper," which really is as simple as it gets. The version we developed for this book tastes like a really good stripped-down mac and cheese—and a single bite takes me back to those Italian dinners and the first few weeks of my pregnancy with my sweet Crew.

8 ounces bucatini pasta

3 tablespoons unsalted butter

1¼ teaspoons freshly cracked black pepper, plus more for garnish

3 ounces Parmesan cheese, grated (about ¾ cup), plus more for garnish

3 ounces pecorino cheese, shredded (about ¾ cup), plus more for garnish

4 boneless, skinless chicken breasts (about 6 ounces each), grilled and cut into 1-inch slices

1. Cook the pasta according to the package directions. Reserving 1 cup of the pasta water, drain the pasta. Set the pasta and cooking water aside.

2. In a large skillet, melt 2 tablespoons of the butter over medium heat. Add the cracked pepper and toast until fragrant, about 30 seconds. Add the pasta cooking water and whisk until well incorporated.

3. Using tongs, add the pasta to the skillet and toss. Add the remaining 1 tablespoon butter and the cheeses and toss until well coated.

4. Serve the pasta in bowls and top each serving with sliced chicken. Garnish with more cheese and cracked pepper and serve.

Makes 4 servings

TIP: *Choose good, high-end cheeses. They make all the difference here.*

Chicken-Fried Steak

WITH BLACK PEPPERCORN GRAVY

prep: *30 minutes*   **cook:** *under 30 minutes*   **cool:** *none*

chicken-fried steak

2 cups all-purpose flour

2 teaspoons seasoned salt

1 teaspoon garlic powder

1 teaspoon freshly ground
   black pepper

½ teaspoon paprika

¼ teaspoon cayenne pepper
   (optional)

3 large eggs

1½ cups whole milk

¼ cup canola oil

3 tablespoons unsalted butter

6 cube steaks (about
   6½ ounces each)

1 teaspoon kosher salt

black peppercorn gravy

¼ cup all-purpose flour

3 cups whole milk

1 teaspoon kosher salt

2 teaspoons black
   peppercorns, freshly
   cracked

1. Preheat the oven to 200°F.

2. To make the chicken-fried steak: Set up a dredging station. In a shallow dish, stir together the flour, seasoned salt, garlic powder, black pepper, paprika, and cayenne (if using). In a second shallow dish, whisk together the eggs and milk.

3. In a large skillet, heat the oil and butter to a bubble over medium heat.

4. Working in an assembly line, dip the tenderized steaks into the flour mixture. Shake off any excess flour and dip in the egg mixture, coating well, then dredge again in the flour. Transfer to a sheet pan. Repeat until all the steaks are coated with the breading. Line a separate sheet pan with foil.

5. Add 3 steaks to the hot skillet and cook until they begin to brown on the edges, 3 to 5 minutes on each side. Remove them to the foil-lined sheet pan, season with ½ teaspoon of the salt while hot, and tent loosely with foil. Repeat with the remaining 3 steaks and remaining ½ teaspoon salt. Place the steaks in the oven to keep warm.

6. To make the black peppercorn gravy: Reduce the heat under the skillet to medium-low and add the flour. Cook, whisking constantly, until the roux is bubbling and lightly colored, 1 to 2 minutes. Whisk the milk into the roux, 1 cup at a time, and stir in the salt and crushed or cracked pepper. Cook, whisking constantly, until the gravy thickens, about 5 minutes.

7. Serve the steaks with the hot gravy on top.

Makes 6 servings

Margherita Pizza

prep: *15 minutes*   **cook:** *under 15 minutes*   **cool:** *none*

The kids love a simple at-home pizza night, especially when they get to customize their toppings. Our go-to lately has been this classic Margherita pizza, but every so often we'll switch it up for something a little more unique, like BBQ Chicken (page 220) or Basil Pesto Chicken (page 221). Each of these pizzas is great for making personal-size pies, and some nights we'll toss them into the oven in a cast-iron skillet, which yields a crust that's equal parts crispy and chewy. We use an 8-inch pan at home, but whatever size pan you have will work fine. Just be sure to adjust the amount of dough you prepare, and keep in mind that the smaller the pan, the thicker the crust.

Homemade Pizza Dough
   (page 29), prepared
   through step 4

¼ cup olive oil

8 ounces fresh mozzarella,
   thinly sliced

2 beefsteak tomatoes (about
   8 ounces each), sliced

½ teaspoon kosher salt

½ teaspoon freshly ground
   black pepper

¼ cup fresh basil leaves

1. Place a cast-iron pizza stone on the center rack of the oven and preheat the oven to 500°F.

2. When the dough has risen, remove the plastic wrap and push down on the dough to release the gases and bubbles. Shape it into a ball. Stretch the dough into a 14-inch round on a sheet of parchment. Drizzle with the olive oil and top evenly with the mozzarella and tomatoes. Sprinkle evenly with the salt and pepper.

3. Transfer the pizza and parchment to the hot pizza stone. Bake until the crust is golden and the cheese is beginning to brown in spots, 13 to 15 minutes.

4. Transfer the pizza to a cutting board, top with the basil, cut into 8 slices, and serve.

Makes 1 pizza, to serve 4

BBQ Chicken Pizza

prep: *20 minutes, plus 30 minutes chilling*   **cook:** *35 minutes*   **cool:** *none*

barbecue sauce

¾ cup ketchup

¼ cup packed dark brown sugar

4 tablespoons (½ stick) salted butter

1 tablespoon yellow mustard

1 tablespoon honey

1 tablespoon apple cider vinegar

1 teaspoon Worcestershire

1½ teaspoons freshly ground black pepper

½ teaspoon crushed red pepper flakes

½ teaspoon paprika

¼ teaspoon onion powder

1 tablespoon olive oil

1 pound boneless, skinless chicken breasts

¾ teaspoon kosher salt

¾ teaspoon freshly ground black pepper

Homemade Pizza Dough (page 29), prepared through step 4

Flour, as needed for the parchment paper

8 ounces sharp Cheddar cheese, grated (about 2 cups)

2 tablespoons unsalted butter, melted

1 teaspoon garlic powder

1. To make the barbecue sauce: In a medium saucepan, combine the ketchup, brown sugar, butter, mustard, honey, vinegar, Worcestershire, black pepper, pepper flakes, paprika, and onion powder. Bring to a low boil over medium-high heat and cook, stirring occasionally, for 2 to 3 minutes. Remove from the heat and cool for 30 minutes. (The sauce can be made ahead and stored in an airtight container in the refrigerator for up to 7 days.)

2. Meanwhile, preheat the oven to 350°F.

3. In a cast-iron skillet, heat the olive oil over medium-high heat. Sprinkle the chicken evenly on both sides with the salt and pepper. Add the chicken to the pan and sear until golden on both sides, 2 to 3 minutes per side. Place the whole skillet in the oven and bake until the chicken is cooked through, about 15 minutes. Transfer the chicken to a bowl to cool slightly, then shred the chicken.

4. Increase the oven temperature to 500°F. Place a cast-iron pizza stone in the oven to preheat for 15 to 20 minutes.

5. When the dough has risen, remove the plastic wrap and push down on the dough to release the gases and bubbles. Shape it into a ball. Stretch the pizza dough to a 14-inch round on a sheet of parchment. (If the dough is sticky, dust it lightly with flour.) Spread ¾ cup of the barbecue sauce over the dough, leaving a ½-inch border. Top with the shredded chicken and Cheddar. Transfer the pizza and parchment to the hot pizza stone.

6. Bake until the crust is golden and the topping is bubbling, 13 to 15 minutes. When the pizza comes out, mix the melted butter and garlic powder and brush it along the crust of the pizza.

7. Transfer to a cutting board and cut into 8 slices to serve.

Makes 1 pizza, to serve 4, and 1½ cups barbecue sauce

Basil Pesto Chicken Pizza

WITH BELL PEPPERS

prep: *20 minutes*   **cook:** *35 minutes*   **cool:** *none*

1 tablespoon olive oil

1 pound boneless, skinless chicken breasts

¾ teaspoon kosher salt

¾ teaspoon freshly ground black pepper

Homemade Pizza Dough (page 29), prepared through step 4

Flour, as needed for the parchment paper

⅓ cup pesto, homemade (see page 37) or store-bought

1 small yellow bell pepper, cut into ¼-inch slices

1 small red bell pepper, cut into ¼-inch slices

4 ounces sharp white Cheddar cheese, grated (about 1 cup)

4 ounces mozzarella cheese, shredded (about 1 cup)

2 tablespoons unsalted butter, melted

1 teaspoon garlic powder

1. Preheat the oven to 350°F.

2. In a cast-iron skillet, heat the olive oil over medium-high heat. Sprinkle the chicken evenly on both sides with the salt and pepper. Add the chicken to the pan and sear until golden on both sides, 2 or 3 minutes per side. Place the whole skillet in the oven and bake until the chicken is cooked through, about 15 minutes. Transfer the chicken to a bowl to cool slightly, then shred the chicken.

3. Increase the oven temperature to 500°F. Place a cast-iron pizza stone in the oven to preheat for 15 to 20 minutes.

4. When the dough has risen, remove the plastic wrap and push down on the dough to release the gases and bubbles. Shape it into a ball. Stretch the pizza dough into a 14-inch round on a sheet of parchment. (If the dough is sticky, dust it lightly with flour.) Spread the pesto over the dough, then layer on the chicken, bell peppers, and shredded cheeses. Transfer the pizza and parchment to the hot pizza stone.

5. Bake until the crust is golden and the topping is bubbling, 13 to 15 minutes. When the pizza comes out, mix the melted butter and garlic powder and brush it along the crust of the pizza.

6. Transfer to a cutting board and cut into 8 slices to serve.

Makes 1 pizza, to serve 4

Brick Paninis

prep: *15 minutes*   **cook:** *under 35 minutes*   **cool:** *none*

1 large garlic clove, halved

8 slices (½ inch thick) rustic white bread, such as sourdough

4 tablespoons (½ stick) butter, melted

margherita

2 large heirloom tomatoes or 4 Roma (plum) tomatoes, thinly sliced

16 ounces fresh mozzarella, cut into ¼-inch-thick slices

Kosher salt and freshly ground black pepper

Leaves from 1 bunch fresh basil

Olive oil, for drizzling

turkey and roasted red pepper

2 tablespoons pesto, homemade (see page 37) or store-bought

1 pound sliced deli roast turkey

One 12-ounce jar roasted red peppers, drained and cut into ½-inch slices

8 slices Fontina or provolone cheese

1. Heat a large skillet or panini press over medium-low heat.

2. Rub the raw garlic clove over both sides of the bread and lightly brush the bread with the melted butter.

3. To make the margherita version: Layer 4 slices of the bread with the tomatoes, then the mozzarella. Season with salt and pepper to taste and top with the basil leaves. Lightly drizzle with olive oil and top with the remaining 4 slices of bread.

4. To make the turkey and roasted pepper version: Spread ½ tablespoon of the pesto on each of 4 slices of bread. Layer on the turkey, roasted peppers, and cheese and top with the remaining 4 slices of bread.

5. Wrap a brick tightly in foil. Place a single sandwich in the skillet and weight down the sandwich with the brick while it cooks through, 3 to 4 minutes per side, returning the brick to the sandwich after you flip it.

6. Slice and serve the sandwiches.

Makes 4 sandwiches

TIP: *If using a panini press, cook each sandwich until melted and toasty according to the manufacturer's instructions.*

Chicken Florentine

prep: *15 minutes*   **cook:** *40 minutes*   **cool:** *none*

2 tablespoons olive oil

4 boneless, skinless chicken breasts (about 6 ounces each)

1 teaspoon freshly ground black pepper

2¾ teaspoons kosher salt

½ cup all-purpose flour

2 tablespoons unsalted butter

½ cup minced shallots (about 2 large)

3 garlic cloves, minced

1 cup good-quality dry white wine

1 cup heavy cream

4 cups baby spinach (about 3 ounces)

1 tablespoon chopped fresh parsley

½ lemon, cut into 4 wedges, for serving

1. In a large skillet, heat the oil over medium-high heat. Sprinkle the chicken with the pepper and 2 teaspoons of the salt. Dredge in the flour, shaking off any excess. Working in batches as needed, place the chicken in the skillet and cook, turning once, until golden brown on both sides and an instant-read thermometer inserted in the thickest part of the meat registers 165°F, about 8 minutes per side. Transfer to a plate to cool and set aside.

2. Reduce the heat to medium and melt the butter in the same skillet. Add the shallots and garlic and sauté, stirring often, until just softened, about 2 minutes. Add the wine, scraping up any browned bits on the bottom of the skillet. Let simmer until the liquid is reduced by half, about 10 minutes. Add the cream and cook, stirring often, until the mixture can coat the back of a spoon, 5 to 8 minutes.

3. Remove the pan from the heat and add the spinach and remaining ¾ teaspoon salt. Stir until the spinach is wilted.

4. Cut the chicken against the grain into diagonal strips 1 inch wide, 2 to 3 inches long, and return it to the skillet. Sprinkle with the parsley and serve with the lemon wedges.

5. Store in an airtight container in the refrigerator for 3 to 5 days.

Makes 4 servings

Seafood Gumbo

prep: *30 minutes*   **cook:** *1 hour*   **cool:** *none*

3 pounds shell-on medium shrimp

2 tablespoons olive oil

1 pound andouille sausage, sliced

1 pound frozen okra, thawed and sliced

3 tablespoons all-purpose flour

6 tablespoons (¾ stick) unsalted butter

1 small yellow onion, diced

2 stalks celery, diced

1 red bell pepper, diced

1 cup drained canned corn

2 garlic cloves, minced

2 tablespoons Creole seasoning

One 28-ounce can crushed tomatoes

6 cups (1½ quarts) shrimp stock (see Note) or store-bought vegetable broth

1 tablespoon Worcestershire

¼ cup loosely packed fresh parsley leaves, chopped

1 pound lump crabmeat

Cooked white or brown rice, for serving

1. Peel the shrimp. If making shrimp stock, reserve the shells and start preparing it now (see Note). If using vegetable broth, discard the shells. Place the shrimp in a bowl and refrigerate.

2. In a large skillet, heat the olive oil over medium-high heat. Add the sausage and sauté until it starts to brown, about 3 minutes. Add the okra and sauté until browned, 5 to 7 minutes more. Remove from the heat and set aside.

3. In a heavy soup pot, combine the flour and butter and cook, stirring constantly, until the roux is light brown, about 2 minutes.

4. Add the onion, celery, bell pepper, corn, and garlic to the roux. Sauté until the onion is translucent and fragrant, 5 to 8 minutes. Stir in the Creole seasoning.

5. Add the tomatoes and shrimp stock or vegetable broth, stir well, and bring to a simmer over medium-high heat. Add the cooked andouille and okra, the Worcestershire, and parsley. Simmer for 25 minutes.

6. Add the shrimp and crabmeat and cook until the shrimp is pink and cooked through, about 5 minutes. Serve over rice.

7. Store the rice and gumbo in separate airtight containers in the refrigerator for up to 2 days.

Makes 10 to 12 servings

NOTE: *If you choose to make shrimp stock, place the shrimp shells in a stockpot and cover with 8 cups cold water. Season with 1 teaspoon each salt and pepper. Bring to a boil over medium-high heat, then reduce to a simmer over medium-low heat. Cover and simmer until fragrant, 15 to 20 minutes. Remove from the heat, strain out and discard the shells, and set the stock aside to cool for about 30 minutes before using.*

Chicken Parmesan

prep: *20 minutes*   **cook:** *25 minutes*   **cool:** *none*

Chicken Parmesan is my favorite dish these days. It's the perfect medley of breaded chicken, marinara sauce, and noodles, and the fact that there seems to be a familiar comfort baked into every bite has me craving this meal again and again.

4 boneless, skinless chicken breasts (about 6 to 8 ounces each)

¼ teaspoon kosher salt

¼ teaspoon freshly ground black pepper

2 large eggs

1 teaspoon garlic salt

1 sleeve (40) buttery crackers, crushed

4 ounces Parmesan cheese, grated (about 1 cup)

2 tablespoons olive oil

1 teaspoon fresh lemon juice

½ cup mayonnaise, preferably Hellmann's

1 tablespoon chopped fresh parsley (optional)

1. Preheat the oven to 400°F.

2. Place the chicken between two sheets of plastic wrap and use a meat pounder or heavy skillet to pound them to a 1-inch thickness to even them out. Season the chicken evenly on both sides with the salt and pepper.

3. In a medium bowl, whisk together the eggs and garlic salt until combined. In another bowl, combine the crackers and ½ cup of the Parmesan. Dredge each chicken breast in the egg mixture, then in the cracker mixture, and set the chicken aside on a plate.

4. In a large skillet, heat 1 tablespoon of the oil over medium heat. Add 2 pieces of the chicken and cook until the cracker coating is crispy and golden brown, 3 or 4 minutes on each side. Remove to a sheet pan. Repeat with the remaining 1 tablespoon oil and chicken breasts.

5. Transfer the sheet pan to the oven and bake until the chicken is cooked through or an instant-read thermometer inserted in the thickest part of the meat registers 165°F, 8 to 10 minutes.

6. Meanwhile, in a medium bowl, combine the remaining ½ cup Parmesan, the lemon juice, and mayonnaise.

7. When the chicken is done, smear it with the mayo/Parmesan topping and turn on the broiler. Broil until the cheese is bubbling and golden, about 3 minutes.

8. Sprinkle with the parsley, if desired, and serve hot.

Makes 4 servings

TIP: *Serve with pasta and marinara sauce.*

Grilled Bruschetta Chicken

prep: *20 minutes*   **cook:** *under 15 minutes*   **cool:** *none*

6 Roma (plum) tomatoes (about 1½ pounds total), diced

½ cup crumbled feta cheese

¼ cup chopped fresh basil leaves

1 teaspoon Greek seasoning

3 tablespoons olive oil

4 boneless, skinless chicken breasts (about 6 ounces each)

½ teaspoon garlic powder

½ teaspoon dried oregano

½ teaspoon kosher salt

½ teaspoon freshly ground black pepper

1. Heat a grill or grill pan to medium-high heat (about 350°F).

2. In a medium bowl, combine the tomatoes, feta, basil, Greek seasoning, and 1½ tablespoons of the olive oil and stir gently to mix. Set the bruschetta mixture aside to let the flavors meld.

3. Pat the chicken dry with paper towels and place it on a sheet pan.

4. In a small bowl, mix together the garlic powder, oregano, salt, and pepper. Sprinkle evenly over the chicken. Drizzle the remaining 1½ tablespoons olive oil over the top. Use your hands to rub the mixture into the chicken breasts, coating well.

5. Grill the chicken until an instant-read thermometer inserted in the thickest part of the meat registers 165°F, 8 to 12 minutes, turning halfway through the cooking time. Set aside to rest for 2 to 3 minutes.

6. Serve the grilled chicken hot, with the bruschetta mixture spooned on top right before serving.

7. Store in an airtight container in the refrigerator for up to 2 days.

Makes 4 servings

Honey Garlic Chicken

WITH PINEAPPLE

prep: *15 minutes*   **cook:** *35 minutes*   **cool:** *none*

½ cup apple cider vinegar

½ cup honey

1 cup ketchup

4 tablespoons (½ stick) unsalted butter, melted

2 teaspoons garlic salt

2 garlic cloves, minced

8 boneless, skinless chicken thighs (about 4 ounces each)

1 tablespoon vegetable oil

½ teaspoon kosher salt

½ teaspoon freshly ground black pepper

2 cups cubed (1 inch) fresh pineapple

1½ cups red bell pepper strips (about 2 large)

1 tablespoon minced fresh parsley

1 tablespoon toasted sesame seeds

Cooked rice, for serving

1. Position an oven rack 6 inches from the broiler element and preheat the oven to 400°F.

2. In a medium bowl, whisk together the vinegar, honey, ketchup, melted butter, garlic salt, and garlic until well combined.

3. Place the chicken thighs on one side of a sheet pan and pat them dry. Drizzle with the oil and sprinkle with the salt and pepper. Bake for 15 minutes.

4. Remove from the oven and place the pineapple and bell peppers on the other end of the pan. Baste the chicken thighs with ½ cup of the sauce and bake for 10 minutes.

5. Turn the oven to broil (do not remove the pan) and broil until the chicken is charred in several places, 8 to 10 minutes.

6. Transfer the chicken, pineapple, and peppers to a large bowl and toss with ½ cup of the remaining sauce.

7. Top with fresh parsley and sesame seeds. Serve over rice with the remaining sauce on the side.

8. Store in an airtight container in the refrigerator for 3 to 5 days.

Makes 4 servings

Weeknight Salmon

WITH BABY NEW POTATOES AND FRESH DILL

prep: *15 minutes*　　**cook:** *25 minutes*　　**cool:** *none*

1 pound baby new potatoes, quartered

2 tablespoons olive oil

1 teaspoon garlic salt

1 teaspoon kosher salt

1 teaspoon freshly ground black pepper

1 teaspoon paprika

1 teaspoon onion powder

4 skin-on salmon fillets, 1½ inches thick (about 8 ounces each)

3 tablespoons unsalted butter, melted

2 Meyer lemons

1 tablespoon chopped fresh dill

1 tablespoon chopped fresh parsley

1. Preheat the oven to 425°F.

2. In a large bowl, toss together the potatoes, olive oil, and ½ teaspoon each of the garlic salt and kosher salt. Arrange the potatoes on one end of a nonstick sheet pan or a sheet pan lined with foil.

3. Roast until the potatoes are tender and golden on the bottom, about 15 minutes, turning them once with a spatula during cooking.

4. Meanwhile, in a small bowl, mix together the pepper, paprika, onion powder, and remaining ½ teaspoon each garlic salt and kosher salt.

5. Cut two 1-inch-long, ¼-inch-deep slits in the fleshy side of each fillet for the butter and seasonings to seep in. Place the salmon fillets on the empty side of the sheet pan, skin side down. Drizzle the melted butter over the salmon and potatoes. Sprinkle the spice mixture over the top. Cut a lemon in half and squeeze both halves over the entire sheet pan, capturing the seeds in your hand.

6. Bake until the salmon flakes with a fork, 10 to 12 minutes.

7. Cut the remaining lemon into 4 wedges. Sprinkle the salmon and potatoes with the dill and parsley and serve with the lemon wedges.

8. Store in an airtight container in the refrigerator for 1 to 3 days.

Makes 4 servings

Cajun Shrimp

SHEET PAN DINNER

prep: *15 minutes* **cook:** *under 50 minutes* **cool:** *none*

1½ pounds baby red or multicolored potatoes, halved

2 tablespoons olive oil

¾ teaspoon kosher salt

¾ teaspoon freshly ground black pepper

4 ears corn, husked and cut crosswise into 1-inch rounds

3 garlic heads, tops sliced off to expose the cloves, plus 4 garlic cloves, minced

8 tablespoons (1 stick) unsalted butter, melted

2 tablespoons Old Bay seasoning

2 pounds medium shrimp, peeled and deveined

2 tablespoons chopped fresh parsley

1 large lemon, cut into wedges, for serving

1. Preheat the oven to 425°F. Line a sheet pan with foil.

2. In a large bowl, combine the potatoes, 1 tablespoon of the olive oil, and ½ teaspoon each of the salt and pepper. Stir to coat.

3. Spread the potatoes evenly on the prepared sheet pan. Roast until the potatoes begin to brown and soften, about 25 minutes.

4. Meanwhile, in the same bowl, combine the corn and garlic heads with the remaining 1 tablespoon oil and ¼ teaspoon each salt and pepper.

5. Add the corn and garlic heads, cut sides up, to the pan with the potatoes and roast for 15 minutes more.

6. In a small bowl, stir together the minced garlic, melted butter, and Old Bay.

7. Remove the pan from the oven and spread the shrimp over the vegetables. Drizzle the butter mixture over the shrimp and vegetables and roast until the shrimp are pink and no longer translucent, 5 to 7 minutes more.

8. Sprinkle the shrimp and vegetables with the parsley and serve immediately with the lemon wedges.

Makes 4 to 6 servings

Braised Short Ribs

WITH HOMEMADE GNOCCHI

prep: *20 minutes*   **cook:** *under 5 hours*   **cool:** *none*

2 tablespoons canola oil

4 pounds bone-in short ribs
 (8 to 12 small or 4 to
 6 large)

1 tablespoon kosher salt

1 medium yellow onion, cut
 into medium dice

3 large carrots, cut into
 ½-inch slices

4 celery stalks, cut into
 medium dice

2 garlic cloves, minced

1 cup dry red wine

4 cups beef broth

5 thyme sprigs

½ teaspoon freshly ground
 black pepper

1 tablespoon chopped fresh
 parsley, for garnish

Homemade Gnocchi
 (page 34), for serving

1. In a large Dutch oven, heat the oil over medium-high heat. Sprinkle the short ribs with 2 teaspoons of the salt. Add the ribs to the pan (working in batches as needed) and sear each side until browned, 3 to 5 minutes per side, 12 to 15 minutes total. Remove the short ribs to a bowl, cover with foil to keep them warm, and set aside.

2. Add the onion, carrots, celery, and garlic to the pot. Sauté, stirring occasionally, until the onion is translucent, about 5 minutes.

3. Add the wine to the pot, scraping any browned bits from the bottom of the pan. Cook until the wine is reduced to ¼ cup, 4 to 5 minutes. Add the beef broth and thyme, bring to a low boil, and reduce the heat to a simmer.

4. Return the short ribs to the pot, with any juices from the bowl. Cover and simmer until fork tender, 4½ to 5 hours.

5. Remove the ribs to a bowl and tent with foil to keep warm. Strain the liquid.

6. Pour the liquid into a medium saucepan and simmer over high heat until slightly thickened and reduced to 1 cup, 8 to 10 minutes. Stir in the remaining 1 teaspoon salt and the pepper.

7. Spoon the sauce over the ribs and sprinkle with the parsley. Serve with gnocchi.

8. Store in an airtight container in the refrigerator for up to 3 days.

Makes 4 to 6 servings

TIP: *To make gravy for the gnocchi, in step 6, whisk ¼ cup cornstarch into ½ cup water and add it to the cooking liquid. Cook until thickened, about 5 minutes.*

White Vegetable Lasagna

prep: *40 minutes*   **cook:** *1 hour 25 minutes*   **cool:** *none*

15 lasagna noodles (most of a 16-ounce box)

2 tablespoons olive oil

8 ounces cremini mushrooms, thickly sliced

1 tablespoon minced garlic

Cooking spray

8 ounces shredded Parmesan cheese (about 2 cups)

1 cup heavy cream

¼ cup loosely packed fresh basil leaves, chopped, plus 1 tablespoon leaves for garnish

1 tablespoon garlic salt

1 teaspoon kosher salt

2 teaspoons freshly ground black pepper

One 24-ounce tub small-curd cottage cheese

16 ounces whole-milk ricotta

3 large eggs

2 medium zucchini, sliced into ⅛-inch-thick ribbons with a vegetable peeler

2 medium yellow squash, sliced into ⅛-inch-thick ribbons with a vegetable peeler

18 deli slices mozzarella cheese

12 ounces shredded Italian five-cheese blend (about 3 cups)

1. Cook the noodles according to the package directions. Drain.

2. Heat a large sauté pan over medium-high heat. Add the olive oil, mushrooms, and garlic and sauté until the mushrooms are tender and just starting to brown, about 5 minutes. Remove from the heat and set aside to cool for at least 5 minutes.

3. Preheat the oven to 350°F. Spray a deep lasagna pan (9 × 13 × 3 inches) with cooking spray.

4. In a large bowl, combine the Parmesan, cream, chopped basil, garlic salt, kosher salt, pepper, cottage cheese, ricotta, and eggs. Mix well, then stir in the mushrooms.

5. Spread ½ cup of the cheese/mushroom mixture to cover the bottom of the lasagna pan.

6. Make the following layers: 5 noodles, 2 cups of the cheese/mushroom mixture, half of the zucchini and squash, 6 mozzarella slices, and 1 cup Italian cheese blend.

7. Repeat step 6.

8. Top with a final layer of 5 noodles, 2 cups of the cheese/mushroom mixture, 6 mozzarella slices, and 1 cup Italian cheese blend.

9. Cover the pan with foil. Bake for 1 hour, then remove the foil and bake until the top is browned, about 20 minutes longer.

10. Sprinkle with the basil and serve.

11. Store, covered, in the refrigerator for 3 to 5 days.

Makes 12 servings

Dutch Oven Lasagna

prep: *30 minutes*   **cook:** *2 hours 10 minutes*   **cool:** *30 minutes*

2 pounds ground chuck (80% lean)

1½ cups small-diced white onion (about 1 small)

1 tablespoon garlic powder

1 tablespoon Italian seasoning

1½ teaspoons kosher salt

1 teaspoon freshly ground black pepper

Four 14.5-ounce cans stewed or roasted diced tomatoes, undrained

4 garlic cloves, minced

½ cup loosely packed fresh basil leaves, torn

One 8-ounce block cream cheese, at room temperature

8 ounces whole-milk ricotta

2 large eggs

16 ounces mozzarella cheese, shredded (about 4 cups)

12 uncooked lasagna noodles

4 fresh mozzarella balls (4 ounces each), torn into 1- to 2-inch chunks

1. In a 7-quart Dutch oven, sauté the beef and onion over medium-high heat until the beef is browned and cooked through, about 6 minutes. Drain the extra fat from the pan.

2. Stir in the garlic powder, Italian seasoning, salt, and pepper. Add the tomatoes, fresh garlic, and basil and break the tomatoes into small pieces with a wooden spoon. Bring to a boil over high heat, reduce the heat to low, and simmer for 20 minutes. Reserve two-thirds of the meat mixture (about 6 cups) in a large bowl.

3. Preheat the oven to 325°F.

4. In a separate large bowl, combine the cream cheese, ricotta, eggs, and 2 cups of the mozzarella.

5. Spread the remaining meat mixture evenly in the Dutch oven. Lay 4 of the lasagna noodles on top (break them as needed to fit). Top with one-third of the ricotta mixture and one-third of the freshly torn mozzarella.

6. Repeat the layers two more times, using half of the reserved meat mixture in each layer. Top with the remaining 2 cups shredded mozzarella.

7. Cover the Dutch oven, transfer to the oven, and bake for 1 hour 30 minutes. Uncover and bake until the cheese is browned and bubbling, about 15 minutes longer.

8. Let the lasagna stand at least 30 minutes before serving to allow the dish to set, making for a cleaner serving.

9. Store, covered, in the refrigerator for up to 5 days.

Makes 12 servings

Rib Eye Steaks

prep: *10 minutes*   **cook:** *under 15 minutes*   **cool:** *none*

Chip and I have made a tradition of spending Valentine's Day dinner with the kids. Every year, we all pitch in to prepare a really good meal, and everyone loves to dress up. I'll set the table with pretty plates and linens and we all eat by candlelight. It's become a yearly ritual of ours to spend this day celebrating the love we share as a family. Some years we'll switch up the menu slightly, but Chip always makes a variation of this rib eye, served with fettuccine, salad, bread, and of course, dessert. This is always a meal we look forward to sharing and one of our family's favorite traditions.

1 tablespoon canola oil

4 rib eye steaks (8 ounces each), patted dry with paper towels

1 teaspoon kosher salt

1 teaspoon freshly ground black pepper

4 tablespoons Becki's Herb Butter (page 53)

Roasted Rosemary Sweet Potatoes (page 170), for serving

1. Preheat the oven to 350°F.

2. In a large ovenproof skillet, heat the oil over medium-high heat until shimmering. Season both sides of the steaks with the salt and pepper. Add the steaks to the pan and sear until browned on both sides, 3 to 4 minutes per side. (If your skillet isn't large enough to hold all 4 steaks comfortably, cook the steaks in batches and tent with foil on a sheet pan to keep warm.)

3. Transfer the skillet to the oven to finish cooking to desired doneness, 5 to 7 minutes for medium-rare, 10 to 12 minutes for well done.

4. Top each steak with 1 tablespoon of the herb butter. Let it melt slightly before serving with the sweet potatoes.

Makes 4 servings

Chicken Street Tacos

prep: *15 minutes*   **cook:** *under 40 minutes*   **cool:** *5 minutes*

shredded chicken

1 teaspoon chili powder

1 teaspoon ground cumin

1 teaspoon kosher salt

½ teaspoon garlic powder

½ teaspoon freshly ground
   black pepper

½ teaspoon smoked paprika

6 boneless, skinless chicken
   breasts (6 to 8 ounces
   each)

½ cup chicken broth

tacos

One 15.25-ounce can corn
   kernels, drained

½ cup crumbled Cotija cheese

½ cup Pickled Red Onion
   (page 165)

¼ cup chopped fresh cilantro

Juice of 2 small limes

1 teaspoon chili powder

1 teaspoon kosher salt

½ teaspoon freshly ground
   black pepper

8 to 10 corn tortillas,
   homemade (see page 31) or
   store-bought

1. To make the shredded chicken: Preheat the oven to 375°F.

2. In a small bowl, mix together the chili powder, cumin, salt, garlic powder, pepper, and smoked paprika.

3. Place the chicken breasts in a 9 × 13-inch baking dish and season them all over with the spice mixture. Slowly pour the chicken broth onto the bottom of the dish (so as not to disturb the spices) and cover with foil.

4. Bake until cooked through, 35 to 40 minutes. Set aside to cool for approximately 5 minutes, then shred the chicken with forks and return it to the juices in the baking dish until ready to serve.

5. To make the tacos: In a medium bowl, stir together the corn, Cotija, pickled red onion, cilantro, lime juice, chili powder, salt, and pepper.

6. In a medium skillet over medium-high heat, char the tortillas for 1 minute on each side, until browning begins. You want the tortillas to still be malleable, not hard or crispy.

7. Layer the chicken and corn mixture in the tortillas and serve.

Makes 4 or 5 servings

TIP: *Serve with Cilantro Lime Rice (page 171).*

Steak Tacos

WITH MEXICAN CREMA

prep: *40 minutes, plus 10 minutes chilling*   **cook:** *under 12 minutes*   **cool:** *none*

steak

2 pounds skirt steak

1 tablespoon fajita seasoning

½ tablespoon canola oil

mexican crema

½ cup sour cream

¼ cup heavy cream

1½ tablespoons adobo sauce
(from canned chipotle
peppers)

2 teaspoons fresh lime juice

⅛ teaspoon kosher salt

tacos

½ cup julienned radishes,
cut into ¼-inch-thick
matchsticks (12 to 14 small)

1 tablespoon finely chopped
fresh cilantro

1 tablespoon thinly sliced
green onion

1 tablespoon fresh lime juice

½ tablespoon cooking oil

¼ teaspoon kosher salt

⅛ teaspoon freshly ground
black pepper

8 or 10 corn tortillas,
homemade (see page 31) or
store-bought, warmed

1. To make the steak: Rub the skirt steak with the fajita seasoning and oil and let the steak sit until it comes to room temperature.

2. In a large skillet, cook the steak over medium-high heat until seared and browned, 5 to 6 minutes per side. Remove to a cutting board to rest for 10 minutes before slicing into thin strips.

3. To make the Mexican crema: In a small bowl, whisk together the sour cream, heavy cream, adobo sauce, lime juice, and salt until well combined. Refrigerate for 10 minutes before serving.

4. Store in an airtight container in the refrigerator for up to 3 days.

5. Meanwhile, to make the tacos: In a medium bowl, toss together the radishes, cilantro, green onion, lime juice, oil, salt, and pepper and let marinate for 10 minutes.

6. While the radishes marinate, in a medium skillet over medium-high heat, char the tortillas for 1 minute on each side, until browning begins. You want the tortillas to still be malleable, not hard or crispy.

7. Layer the steak, crema, and radish salsa on the tortillas and serve.

Makes 4 or 5 servings

Pulled Pork Street Tacos

prep: *20 minutes*   **cook:** *6 to 8 hours*   **cool:** *none*

pulled pork

2 tablespoons light brown sugar

½ tablespoon ground cumin

½ tablespoon chili powder

1 teaspoon onion powder

1 teaspoon garlic powder

1 teaspoon mustard powder

1½ teaspoons kosher salt

1 teaspoon freshly ground black pepper

3 pounds boneless pork shoulder or butt, trimmed

1 cup apple juice

tacos

2 ounces Cheddar cheese, grated (about ½ cup)

¼ small red onion, thinly sliced

½ cup roughly chopped fresh cilantro

½ cup Jo's Salsa (see *Magnolia Table, Volume 1*) or salsa of your choice

8 to 10 corn tortillas, homemade (see page 31) or store-bought

1. To make the pulled pork: In a medium bowl, mix the brown sugar, cumin, chili powder, onion powder, garlic powder, mustard powder, salt, and pepper. Rub the pork with the seasoning mixture until well coated.

2. Place the pork in a slow cooker and pour the apple juice and 1 cup water on top. Cover and cook on low for 6 to 8 hours, until the pork shreds easily with a fork.

3. Place the pork on a platter and shred all the meat with two forks. Return the meat to the slow cooker with its juices and keep warm until ready to use (or refrigerate the pork in its juices and reheat when ready).

4. To make the tacos: In a medium skillet over medium-high heat, char the tortillas for 1 minute on each side, until browning begins. You want the tortillas to still be malleable, not hard or crispy.

5. Layer the pulled pork, Cheddar, onion, cilantro, and salsa on the tortillas and serve.

Makes 4 or 5 servings

Monte Cristo Sandwiches

prep: *30 minutes*   **cook:** *1 hour 5 minutes*   **cool:** *none*

It's no surprise to me that my all-time favorite sandwich happens to be battered and fried. There are a lot of variations of this Southern classic, but my absolute favorite way to eat a Monte Cristo is with a side of raspberry jelly and topped with powdered sugar. There's something about that sweet and salty combination that just can't be beat.

batter

3⅔ cups all-purpose flour

¼ cup granulated sugar

2 teaspoons baking powder

½ teaspoon kosher salt

3 large eggs

3 cups milk

sandwiches

16 ounces Gruyère cheese, shredded (about 4 cups)

16 slices white sandwich bread

16 slices deli ham

16 slices deli turkey

to finish

Vegetable oil, for deep-frying

⅓ cup powdered sugar

1 cup seedless raspberry preserves

1. To make the batter: In a medium bowl, whisk together the flour, granulated sugar, baking powder, and salt. Add the eggs and milk and whisk until smooth. Set aside.

2. To make each sandwich: Sprinkle about ¼ cup of the Gruyère over 1 slice of bread. Top with 2 slices ham and 2 slices turkey, then sprinkle ¼ cup Gruyère over the meat. Place a second slice of bread on top.

3. To finish: Pour 3 inches of oil into a deep saucepan or Dutch oven. Have ready a wire rack lined with paper towels to use for draining. Heat the oil to 350°F on a deep-fry thermometer.

4. Working with 1 sandwich at a time, carefully dip it in the batter, letting the excess batter drip back into the bowl.

5. Slowly lower a battered sandwich into the oil and fry until golden brown on the bottom, about 4 minutes. Using a spatula, flip the sandwich over and fry until golden brown on the other side, about 4 minutes. Remove the sandwich to the paper towel–lined rack to absorb the excess grease. Repeat to fry the remaining sandwiches.

6. Using a sifter or fine-mesh sieve, gently tap 2 teaspoons of the powdered sugar over each sandwich.

7. In a small, microwave-safe bowl, stir together the raspberry preserves and 2 teaspoons water. Microwave on high for 30 seconds, until loosened.

8. Serve each sandwich with about 2 tablespoons raspberry preserves for dipping.

Makes 8 sandwiches

Beef Stroganoff

prep: *20 minutes*   **cook:** *40 minutes*   **cool:** *none*

I loved beef stroganoff as a kid, so when we started developing recipes for this book, I knew I wanted to include a whole-ingredient version of this childhood favorite of mine. At home, I'll serve it with dinner rolls, just like my mom used to, and it's always an easy win for our family of seven.

12 ounces egg noodles

1½ pounds top sirloin or New York strip steak, cut into 1- to 2-inch cubes

1½ teaspoons kosher salt

1½ teaspoons freshly ground black pepper

1 teaspoon garlic powder

3 tablespoons all-purpose flour

4 tablespoons (½ stick) unsalted butter

2 tablespoons canola oil

1 small yellow onion, cut into half moons

8 ounces button or cremini mushrooms, cut into ¼-inch slices, or 4 cups sliced mushrooms

1½ cups beef broth

½ cup heavy cream

4 ounces cream cheese, cubed

½ cup sour cream

1 teaspoon chopped fresh thyme leaves (optional)

½ teaspoon Worcestershire

1 tablespoon chopped fresh parsley or chives

1. Bring a large pot of water to a boil and cook the noodles according to the package directions. Drain and set aside.

2. Meanwhile, in large bowl, combine the beef, 1 teaspoon of the salt, 1 teaspoon of the pepper, the garlic powder, and 2 tablespoons of the flour. Toss to coat lightly.

3. In a large skillet, heat 2 tablespoons of the butter and the oil to a sizzle over medium-high heat. Add the beef and sear on all sides, turning as needed, until browned, 7 to 8 minutes. Using a slotted spoon, remove the meat to a bowl. Set aside.

4. Add the onion, mushrooms, and remaining 2 tablespoons of butter to the pan with the drippings and sauté until nicely browned, 6 to 7 minutes. Sprinkle with the remaining 1 tablespoon of flour and stir to coat well. Add the broth and cream and bring to a boil. Reduce the heat to a low simmer, then return the meat to the pan, stir, cover, and cook until the sauce is thickened and coats the back of a spoon, about 5 minutes.

5. Uncover the skillet and add the cream cheese, sour cream, thyme (if using), and Worcestershire. Stir to combine and simmer for 1 minute. Season with the remaining ½ teaspoon salt and ½ teaspoon pepper, stir, and taste for seasoning.

6. To serve, place the noodles on a plate and spoon the stroganoff on top. Sprinkle with the parsley.

7. Store in an airtight container in the refrigerator for 4 to 5 days.

Makes 4 servings

Chicken Puff Pastries

WITH BÉCHAMEL SAUCE

prep: *1 hour*   **cook:** *1 hour 10 minutes*   **cool:** *none*

Two 17.3-ounce packages
  frozen puff pastry

filling

6 slices bacon, cut into
  ¼-inch pieces

3 tablespoons unsalted butter

2 leeks (white parts only),
  thinly sliced

½ small red onion, cut into
  ¼-inch dice

2 green onions, thinly sliced

¼ teaspoon freshly ground
  black pepper

Kosher salt

1 pound shredded cooked
  chicken breast

béchamel sauce

4 tablespoons (½ stick)
  unsalted butter

¼ cup all-purpose flour

2½ cups whole milk, warmed

½ teaspoon kosher salt

¼ teaspoon freshly ground
  black pepper

¼ teaspoon ground nutmeg

assembly

Flour, for the work surface

Kosher salt and freshly ground
  black pepper

1 large egg, whisked

1 tablespoon thinly sliced
  green onions, for garnish

1. Thaw the pastry according to the package directions.

2. In a large skillet, cook the bacon over medium-high heat until crispy, about 8 to 10 minutes. Use a slotted spoon to remove it to a plate lined with paper towels. Drain the grease from the pan.

3. Return the skillet to medium heat and add the butter. Add the leeks and red and green onions and sauté until caramelized, 15 to 20 minutes. Season with the pepper and a pinch of salt. Stir in the bacon and chicken and cook for 2 to 3 minutes to allow the flavors to meld. Set aside in a bowl to cool.

4. In a medium saucepan, melt the butter over medium heat. Add the flour, whisking constantly until a light blond paste forms. Be careful not to burn the roux. Slowly whisk in the warm milk. Bring to a gentle boil, still whisking, until the sauce is thick enough to coat the back of a spoon, 2 to 3 minutes. Whisk in the salt, pepper, and nutmeg. Remove from the heat and whisk for 1 minute; the sauce will emit more steam. Set aside 1 cup of the béchamel, covered, to keep warm.

5. Pour the remaining 1½ cups béchamel over the chicken mixture and stir to combine. Let cool.

6. Preheat the oven to 400°F. Line a sheet pan with foil.

7. Lay out one sheet of the puff pastry on a lightly floured surface. Cut into 4 equal rectangles. Scoop about ½ cup of the chicken mixture onto the center of each piece. Season each with a pinch of salt and pepper.

8. Cut the second puff pastry sheet into 4 equal rectangles and set them on top of each filling. Using your fingers, pinch the edges together to form a seam around the filling. Press the edges with the tines of a fork to add detailing. Repeat with the remaining dough and chicken mixture.

9. Carefully transfer the pastries to the prepared sheet pan, keeping at least 1 inch between. Brush them with the beaten egg. Make a small cut on top of each pastry or poke it with a fork. Season each with a pinch of salt and pepper.

10. Bake until golden brown, 25 to 35 minutes. Serve hot, spooning 2 tablespoons of the reserved béchamel on top of each. Garnish with the green onions. Serve immediately.

Makes 8 servings

Grandpa Stevens' Stuffed Grape Leaves

prep: *30 minutes*   **cook:** *under 50 minutes*   **cool:** *none*

Stuffed grape leaves is a traditional Lebanese meal that my grandfather on my dad's side would make as a Sunday lunch for our entire family. He and my grandmother had nine children and a ton of grandkids, so it was always a big production for him, which made the meal feel like a really big deal. Before my grandpa passed away, he taught my mom the recipe, as well as a version that calls for cabbage, and she has continued to make both a few times a year for my dad—and whenever she does, all of us kids head over. A single bite of my mom's grape leaves and cabbage rolls (page 259) takes me back to those Sunday afternoons sitting around my grandparents' dinner table, surrounded by all of my cousins. My Korean mama has carried on this tradition from my father's heritage as if it were her own, and I just know it would make my grandpa really proud.

1½ pounds ground beef (85% lean)

1 cup uncooked long-grain white rice

¾ cup small-diced sweet onion, such as Vidalia (about 1 small)

½ teaspoon seasoned salt

½ teaspoon Himalayan pink salt

¼ teaspoon freshly ground black pepper

¼ teaspoon garlic powder

⅔ cup tomato juice

One 16-ounce jar grape leaves, drained and rinsed well

1. In a large bowl, combine the ground beef, rice, onion, ¼ teaspoon of the seasoned salt, ¼ teaspoon of the pink salt, ⅛ teaspoon of the pepper, the garlic powder, and ⅓ cup of the tomato juice. Stir to mix well.

2. Use 5 or 6 whole grape leaves to line the bottom of a Dutch oven or medium saucepan.

3. Lay 1 large grape leaf vein side up on a work surface, wide end toward you. Spoon 2 tablespoons of the meat mixture onto the wide end of the leaf. Fold in the sides of the leaf and roll the meat mixture up into the leaf to create a firm package. Place in the pot, seam side down. Repeat with the remaining leaves (reserve 2 or 3) and meat mixture to make about 36 rolls, layering them in the pot as you go. They should touch.

4. In a small bowl, stir together 4 cups water, the remaining ⅓ cup tomato juice, ¼ teaspoon seasoned salt, ¼ teaspoon pink salt, and ⅛ teaspoon pepper. Pour it over the rolls.

5. Place the reserved leaves over the rolls and cover the pot. Set the pot over medium-high heat and bring the liquid to a boil. Reduce the heat to low and simmer until the rice is tender (remove a roll to check), 45 to 50 minutes. Serve warm or at room temperature.

6. Store in a closed container in the refrigerator for up to 3 days.

Makes about 36 rolls

TIP: *My mom serves this dish with a side of either tabbouleh or a Lebanese salad with cucumbers, tomatoes, and pita bread.*

Grandpa Stevens' Cabbage Rolls

prep: *40 minutes, plus 12 hours chilling*   **cook:** *1 hour 50 minutes*   **cool:** *none*

cabbage rolls

1 large head green cabbage

1 pound ground beef
  (80% lean)

½ cup uncooked long-grain
  white rice

½ small sweet onion, such as
  Vidalia, finely diced

½ cup tomato juice

1 teaspoon seasoned salt

½ teaspoon freshly ground
  black pepper

¼ teaspoon Himalayan pink
  salt

¼ teaspoon garlic powder

tomato broth

1 cup tomato juice

1 teaspoon seasoned salt

½ teaspoon Himalayan pink
  salt

½ teaspoon freshly ground
  black pepper

1 lemon, halved, for serving

1. To make the cabbage rolls: Remove and discard the core from the cabbage. Freeze the cabbage for at least 12 hours.

2. Place the frozen cabbage under hot running water, letting it run into the cabbage center. Carefully loosen and peel back each leaf. Repeat until all the leaves are pulled. Place on a baking sheet lined with paper towels and set aside.

3. In a large bowl, combine the beef, rice, onion, tomato juice, seasoned salt, pepper, pink salt, and garlic powder. Using your hands, mix until well combined.

4. Cover the bottom of a Dutch oven or soup pot with a few of the smaller cabbage leaves. (Reserve a few more to lay on top of the rolls.)

5. Hold a cabbage leaf in your hand and place ¼ cup of the meat mixture at the stalk end. Slowly roll up the leaf just until the meat mixture is covered, then fold the sides of the leaf in and continue rolling up the rest of the leaf. Lay the leaf in the pot, seam side down.

6. Repeat with the remaining leaves until the meat mixture is gone, to make about 20 rolls. Stack the rolls in the pot as needed.

7. To make the tomato broth: In a large bowl, combine 3 cups water, the tomato juice, seasoned salt, pink salt, and pepper. Pour the tomato broth over the cabbage rolls. The liquid should come three-quarters of the way up the rolls; if the level is too low, add water to get to that level.

8. Lay the reserved leaves over the rolls and cover the pot. Set the pot over medium-high heat, bring the liquid to a boil, then let it gently boil for 10 minutes. Reduce the heat to medium-low and simmer until the leaves are soft and easy to cut through and the rice is tender (remove a roll to see if the rice is cooked), about 1 hour 30 minutes.

9. Plate 3 or 4 rolls per serving. Squeeze the lemon over the rolls, catching the seeds with your hand.

10. Store in an airtight container in the refrigerator for up to 3 days.

Makes 6 servings

Angel Hair Pasta

WITH LEMON AND WHITE WINE SCAMPI SAUCE

prep: *15 minutes*   **cook:** *25 minutes*   **cool:** *none*

16 ounces angel hair pasta

1 pound thin asparagus, ends trimmed, cut into 2-inch pieces

8 tablespoons (1 stick) unsalted butter

6 garlic cloves, minced

1 pound jumbo shrimp, peeled and deveined

1 teaspoon kosher salt

1 cup good-quality dry white wine

⅓ cup lemon juice (from about 2 lemons)

2 tablespoons chopped fresh parsley, plus more for garnish (optional)

2 tablespoons extra virgin olive oil, for drizzling

1 teaspoon minced dill, for garnish (optional)

1. Cook the pasta according to the package directions, adding the asparagus during the last 2 minutes of cooking. Reserving 1 cup of the cooking water, drain the pasta and asparagus. Set aside in a bowl and cover to keep warm.

2. Meanwhile, in a large skillet, melt 2 tablespoons of the butter over medium-high heat. Add the garlic and sauté until just fragrant, about 30 seconds.

3. Pat the shrimp dry and toss with ½ teaspoon of the salt. Add them to the skillet and sauté until pink and no longer translucent, 3 to 4 minutes. Remove the shrimp to a plate.

4. Add the wine to the pan, scraping any browned bits from the bottom of the pan. Bring to a boil, then simmer until reduced by half, 2 to 3 minutes. Add the lemon juice, shrimp, pasta, asparagus, parsley, the remaining ½ teaspoon salt and 6 tablespoons butter, and ½ cup of the reserved pasta cooking water and toss until combined, adding more pasta water as needed.

5. Divide among bowls and serve immediately, garnished with a swirl of extra virgin olive oil and chopped dill and parsley, if desired.

6. Store in an airtight container in the refrigerator for up to 3 days.

Makes 4 servings

Pulled Brisket Sliders

WITH COLESLAW

prep: *20 minutes*   **cook:** *5 to 6 hours*   **cool:** *none*

1 tablespoon garlic salt

1 tablespoon onion powder

1 teaspoon kosher salt

1 teaspoon freshly ground
   black pepper

6 pounds brisket, fat trimmed

1 tablespoon canola oil

1 large white onion, peeled
   and halved

1 garlic head, halved horizontally

2 cups beef broth

1 cup Worcestershire

¼ cup sweet teriyaki sauce

1 cup barbecue sauce

12 slider buns, split

Coleslaw (page 264)

1. Preheat the oven to 225°F.

2. To make the pulled brisket: In a small bowl, combine the garlic salt, onion powder, kosher salt, and pepper. Rub over both sides of the brisket.

3. Heat a large Dutch oven over medium-high heat. Add the oil and swirl to coat. Add the brisket and cook until browned on both sides, about 6 minutes per side.

4. Settle the brisket in the pan. Add the onion halves, garlic, beef broth, Worcestershire, and teriyaki sauce. Cover and bake in the oven until fork tender, 5 to 6 hours.

5. Let rest for 15 minutes, then shred the meat with 2 forks. Toss with 2 cups of the cooking liquid and the barbecue sauce. Discard any leftover cooking liquid.

6. Store the pork in an airtight container in the refrigerator for 3 to 5 days.

7. To assemble: Place ¼ cup brisket on each bottom bun half. Top with 1½ tablespoons of the slaw and the upper bun halves. Serve immediately.

Makes 6 servings

Coleslaw

prep: *10 minutes*   **cook:** *none*   **cool:** *2 hours*

2 cups shredded rainbow slaw

1 cup shaved Brussels sprouts

1 celery stalk, thinly sliced

4 green onions, thinly sliced

½ cup mayonnaise, preferably
   Hellmann's

2 tablespoons apple cider
   vinegar

½ teaspoon celery seeds

½ teaspoon celery salt

¼ teaspoon paprika

Kosher salt and freshly ground
   black pepper

1. In a large bowl, stir together the slaw, Brussels sprouts, celery, and green onions.

2. In a small bowl, stir together the mayonnaise, vinegar, celery seeds, celery salt, paprika, and salt and pepper to taste.

3. Fold the mayonnaise mixture into the slaw mixture.

4. Refrigerate for 2 hours before serving.

5. Store in an airtight container in the refrigerator for up to 2 days.

Makes 2 cups

TIP: *Serve with Pulled Brisket Sliders (page 263).*

Holiday Cranberry Sauce

prep: *5 minutes, plus 30 minutes chilling*   **cook:** *15 minutes*   **cool:** *2 hours 30 minutes*

3 cups fresh cranberries

1 cup fresh orange juice

1 cup sugar

1 cinnamon stick

1 tablespoon grated orange
   zest

1. In a medium saucepan, combine the cranberries, orange juice, sugar, cinnamon stick, and orange zest. Bring to a boil over medium heat. Reduce the heat to low and cook until thickened and bubbly, stirring constantly, about 3 minutes.

2. Let cool, then remove the cinnamon stick and refrigerate for 2 hours and 30 minutes. Serve chilled.

3. Store in an airtight container in the refrigerator for 4 to 5 days.

Makes 1½ cups

TIP: *Serve with Friendsgiving Casserole (page 267).*

Friendsgiving Casserole

prep: *1 hour 10 minutes*   **cook:** *under 45 minutes*   **cool:** *none*

This is one of my kids' favorite dishes and a go-to of mine when I want to take dinner to a new mother or a family who could use a hot meal—mostly because it's easy to love, even for the pickiest eaters. The chicken is mild in flavor yet completely satisfying. A lot of traditional recipes will serve the chicken on a bed of rice or with a buttery cracker or stuffing-like topping. I prefer to crumble a baguette and bake it right on top, because it never fails to meld oh-so-perfectly with the creamy sauce—which makes it that much easier for a bread-dipping connoisseur like me to get a taste of the good stuff. Often I choose to serve this dish over mashed potatoes and with a side of cranberry sauce and green beans.

1 baguette torn into 1-inch pieces (about 6 cups)

7 tablespoons unsalted butter

½ cup minced yellow onion (1 medium)

½ cup minced celery

1 garlic clove, minced

2 tablespoons all-purpose flour

1 teaspoon garlic salt

1 teaspoon kosher salt

½ teaspoon freshly ground black pepper

1½ cups heavy cream

5 cups shredded cooked chicken breast (home-roasted or rotisserie chicken)

1 cup sour cream

2 cups chicken broth

Freshly cracked black pepper, for garnish

3 green onions, minced (optional)

Chopped fresh parsley (optional)

Holiday Cranberry Sauce (page 265), for serving

1. Lay the torn bread on a sheet pan and place it in a warm oven until dried out, 1 hour on low heat.

2. Increase the oven heat to 325°F.

3. In a medium saucepan, melt 3 tablespoons of the butter over medium heat. Add the onion and celery and sauté until tender and translucent, 6 to 8 minutes.

4. Add the garlic and flour and cook, whisking constantly, until fragrant but not burned, about 1 minute. Add the garlic salt, salt, and pepper and slowly pour in the cream. Cook, whisking often, until just at a simmer, about 5 minutes.

5. Spread the chicken in a 9 × 13-inch baking dish and spread the sour cream on top. Pour the cream sauce evenly on top and sprinkle on the bread pieces. Melt the remaining 4 tablespoons butter, mix in the chicken broth, and pour it over the casserole, coating the bread well.

6. Bake, uncovered, until bubbling, about 30 minutes. Broil the last 3 to 4 minutes for a good toasty top. Top with freshly cracked pepper and a sprinkle of minced green onions and parsley, if desired.

7. Scoop out the casserole to serve with cranberry sauce on the side.

8. Store in an airtight container in the refrigerator for 3 to 5 days.

Makes 8 to 10 servings

Ham & Swiss Stuffed Chicken Roulades

prep: *15 minutes* **cook:** *under 45 minutes* **cool:** *none*

4 boneless, skinless chicken breasts (about 6 to 8 ounces each)

½ teaspoon garlic powder

2 tablespoons chiffonade-cut fresh sage leaves

½ teaspoon kosher salt

½ teaspoon freshly cracked black pepper

4 thick slices ham

4 thick slices Swiss cheese

4 tablespoons (½ stick) unsalted butter, melted

1. Preheat the oven to 375°F.

2. Place the chicken breasts between two sheets of plastic wrap and use a meat pounder or heavy skillet to gently pound them to a ¼-inch thickness.

3. Sprinkle the chicken evenly with the garlic powder, sage, and ¼ teaspoon each of the salt and pepper. Cover each breast with a slice of ham and a slice of cheese.

4. Starting on a long side, tightly roll up each breast and secure it with toothpicks to keep it together.

5. Place the rolled breasts in a 9 × 9-inch baking dish. Pour the melted butter over the chicken and season with the remaining ¼ teaspoon each salt and pepper.

6. Cover the dish with foil and bake for 25 minutes. Remove the foil and bake until the chicken is starting to brown and is cooked through, 18 to 20 minutes more.

7. To serve, plate the chicken and use a spoon to drizzle it with the pan juices. Serve whole or sliced to show the filling.

Makes 4 servings

CHAPTER EIGHT

Desserts

DESSERT REMINDS US JUST

HOW SWEET LIFE CAN BE

Peach Cobbler

SERVED AT
magnolia table
WACO · TX

prep: *15 minutes*   **cook:** *50 minutes*   **cool:** *none*

4 cups sliced peeled fresh or frozen peaches

1¾ cups sugar

1 cup all-purpose flour

1 tablespoon baking powder

1 teaspoon kosher salt

¾ cup whole milk

8 tablespoons (1 stick) unsalted butter

½ teaspoon ground cinnamon

Vanilla ice cream, for serving

1. In a large saucepan, combine the peaches and ¾ cup of the sugar. Cook over medium heat, stirring often, until the sugar dissolves, the juice is thickened, and the peaches are softened but still firm, 8 to 10 minutes.

2. In a large bowl, whisk together the flour, remaining 1 cup sugar, baking powder, and salt. Stir in the milk and mix until combined.

3. Place the butter in an 8 × 8-inch baking dish and set it in the oven. Preheat the oven to 350°F. Take out the dish when the butter has melted, 3 to 5 minutes.

4. Pour the batter into the dish on top of the melted butter. Spoon the peaches and juice over the batter and sprinkle the cinnamon on top.

5. Bake until a tester inserted in the center comes out clean, about 35 minutes. Serve warm with ice cream.

Makes 6 servings

Lucy's Peanut Butter Brownies

prep: *15 minutes, plus 30 minutes cooling and 1 hour freezing*   **cook:** *under 35 minutes*   **cool:** *none*

"Best friend brownies" is what my friend's mom, Lucy, calls this sweet treat. Anytime a friend of hers is feeling down or could just use a little something sweet, she makes a batch. Over the years, many of her friends have asked her for the recipe so they could do the same. I'm grateful to share it here, as I am convinced there is no better match than peanut butter and chocolate.

brownies

Cooking spray

1 cup (2 sticks) unsalted butter

⅓ cup unsweetened cocoa powder

2 cups granulated sugar

1½ cups all-purpose flour

½ teaspoon kosher salt

4 large eggs

1 teaspoon pure vanilla extract

topping

One 16-ounce jar creamy peanut butter

frosting

8 tablespoons (1 stick) unsalted butter

10 large marshmallows

4 cups powdered sugar, or more for a thicker frosting

⅓ cup whole milk

¼ cup unsweetened cocoa powder

1. To make the brownies: Preheat the oven to 350°F. Spray a 9 × 13-inch pan well with cooking spray.

2. In a small saucepan, combine the butter and cocoa. Set over low heat until the butter melts, then whisk together with the cocoa. Set aside to cool, approximately 5 minutes.

3. In a stand mixer fitted with the paddle attachment, combine the granulated sugar, flour, and salt. Add the cocoa/butter mixture and beat on medium speed until well blended, about 2 minutes. Slowly add the eggs and vanilla and mix until well incorporated.

4. Spread the mixture evenly in the prepared pan. Bake until a tester inserted into the center comes out with a few moist crumbs, 20 to 22 minutes.

5. Let the brownies cool completely, about 30 minutes.

6. To make the topping: Soften the peanut butter by placing it in a microwave-safe bowl and microwave for about 15 seconds. Stir the peanut butter well to distribute the heat evenly. Spread it on top of the brownies. Freeze the brownies for at least 30 minutes.

7. To make the frosting: In a medium saucepan, melt the butter and marshmallows over medium heat. Add the powdered sugar, milk, and cocoa and stir until smooth. (For a thicker frosting, add a little more powdered sugar.)

8. Spread the frosting over the peanut butter and freeze for 30 minutes.

9. Cut into 24 squares. Keep refrigerated.

Makes 24 servings

Baklava

prep: *40 minutes*   **cook:** *under 45 minutes*   **cool:** *at least 4 hours*

1½ cups (8 ounces) whole raw almonds, toasted

1⅔ cups (8 ounces) raw pistachios, plus 3 tablespoons chopped toasted pistachios

¼ cup sugar

1 teaspoon ground cardamom

1 teaspoon ground cinnamon

¼ teaspoon ground nutmeg

¼ teaspoon kosher salt

1¼ cups (2½ sticks) unsalted butter, melted

One 16-ounce package frozen phyllo dough, thawed

honey syrup

¾ cup sugar

1 cup good-quality raw honey

One 3-inch strip orange peel (with pith)

1 tablespoon fresh orange juice

1. Preheat the oven to 350°F.

2. In a food processor, combine the almonds, the 1⅔ cups of pistachios, the sugar, cardamom, cinnamon, nutmeg, and salt and pulse until finely chopped, about 12 times, leaving some of the nuts in larger pieces.

3. Brush a 9 × 13-inch baking pan generously with some of the melted butter. Lay the phyllo sheets on a piece of plastic wrap and cover with another piece of plastic wrap followed by a damp towel. Place 1 sheet of phyllo on the bottom of the prepared pan and trim it to fit. Brush generously with melted butter and repeat with 5 more sheets of phyllo, gently pressing them on top of each other.

4. Sprinkle with one-third of the nut mixture (about 1 cup). Top the nut mixture with a phyllo sheet and brush it generously with butter. Repeat with 5 more phyllo sheets.

5. Repeat with another one-third of the nut mixture and 6 phyllo sheets, brushing each with butter. Sprinkle with the remaining nut mixture.

6. Top with 10 phyllo sheets, brushing each sheet generously with butter. (Reserve the remaining phyllo for another use.)

7. Using a sharp knife, cut the phyllo layers into 24 (about 2¼-inch) squares. Cut each square in half on the diagonal. Bake until golden brown, 40 to 45 minutes. Set the baklava pan on a wire rack.

8. Meanwhile, make the honey syrup: (The syrup should be ready when the baklava comes out of the oven.) In a medium saucepan, combine the sugar, honey, 1 cup of water, and the orange peel. Bring the mixture to a boil over medium-high heat, stirring occasionally. Reduce the heat to medium-low and simmer, stirring occasionally, until slightly thickened, about 10 minutes. Remove from the heat and stir in the orange juice. Discard the orange peel.

9. Slowly pour all the warm syrup over the hot baklava, covering the entire surface. Sprinkle the 3 tablespoons of chopped toasted pistachios on top.

10. Let stand at room temperature on a wire rack at least 4 hours or up to overnight before serving.

11. Store in an airtight container at room temperature for up to 3 days.

Makes 24 servings

French Silk Pie

prep: *20 minutes,*
plus at least 4 hours chilling

cook: *10 minutes*

cool: *20 minutes (for the*
chocolate cookie crust)

French silk pie is a tried-and-true classic that's typically served with a traditional pie crust. I am a firm believer that the more chocolate the better, so I often make this pie with a chocolate cookie crust for an even richer flavor.

⅔ cup granulated sugar

2 large eggs

2 ounces unsweetened chocolate, chopped

1 teaspoon pure vanilla extract

⅓ cup (⅔ stick) unsalted butter, at room temperature

⅔ cup heavy cream

¼ cup powdered sugar

1 prebaked 9-inch pie crust or tart shell (as shown) or Chocolate Cookie Crust (see below)

Whipped cream (see page 321) and shaved dark chocolate (optional), for garnish

1. In a small saucepan, whisk together the granulated sugar and eggs until well blended. Cook over low heat, whisking constantly, until the mixture reaches 160°F and coats the back of a metal spoon. Remove from the heat. Add the chocolate and vanilla and stir until smooth. Set aside to cool for approximately 5 minutes.

2. In a stand mixer fitted with the paddle attachment, cream the butter on medium-high speed until light and fluffy. Add the cooled chocolate mixture and beat on high speed until light and fluffy, about 5 minutes.

3. In another large bowl, beat the cream on medium-high speed until it begins to thicken, 3 to 4 minutes. Add the powdered sugar and beat on low speed, then gradually return to medium-high until stiff peaks form. Fold into the chocolate mixture.

4. Pour into the prebaked pie crust or tart shell. Refrigerate until well chilled, at least 4 hours or up to overnight.

5. Garnish with whipped cream and shaved chocolate, if desired.

6. Store, covered, in the refrigerator for 4 to 5 days.

Makes one 9-inch pie or tart

chocolate cookie crust (optional)

5 ounces chocolate wafers

¼ cup sugar

8 tablespoons (1 stick) butter, melted

chocolate cookie crust

1. Preheat the oven to 350°F.

2. Pulse the wafers on low in a food processor until they are the consistency of sand. Add the sugar and melted butter and mix well.

3. Press the mixture into the bottom and up the sides of a 9-inch pie pan. Bake 8 minutes.

4. Let cool 20 minutes before filling.

Naked Coconut Cake

prep: *35 minutes, plus 55 minutes cooling*   **cook:** *under 40 minutes*   **cool:** *none*

cake batter

1½ cups (3 sticks) unsalted butter, at room temperature

3 cups granulated sugar

6 large eggs

2 teaspoons coconut extract

3 cups all-purpose flour

1 tablespoon kosher salt

1 tablespoon baking powder

1½ cups buttermilk

Nonstick baking spray

topping

1½ cups sweetened shredded coconut

coconut icing

1 cup (2 sticks) unsalted butter, at room temperature

1 cup vegetable shortening

1 teaspoon kosher salt

2 teaspoons coconut extract

3 cups powdered sugar, sifted

3 tablespoons milk

1. Preheat the oven to 350°F.

2. To make the cake batter: In a stand mixer fitted with the paddle attachment, cream the butter and sugar until light and fluffy. In a small bowl, combine the eggs and coconut extract. With the mixer on low speed, slowly add the egg mixture, then kick the mixer up to medium-high to better incorporate.

3. In a medium bowl, whisk together the flour, salt, and baking powder. With the mixer on low speed, alternate adding the buttermilk and the flour mixture, starting with half the buttermilk, then half the flour, then repeat.

4. To bake the cake: Spray three 9-inch round pans with nonstick baking spray. Line the bottoms of the pans with rounds of parchment paper and spray with nonstick baking spray. Divide the batter evenly among the pans. Bake until a tester inserted in the center comes out clean, 25 to 30 minutes. (Leave the oven on for toasting the coconut.) Let the cakes cool in the pans for 10 minutes, then carefully unmold them onto wire racks and peel off the parchment paper. Set aside to cool completely before frosting, about 45 minutes.

5. Meanwhile, make the topping: Spread the shredded coconut on a sheet pan and toast in the oven until it begins to brown, 5 to 7 minutes.

6. To make the coconut icing: In a stand mixer fitted with the paddle attachment, cream the butter and shortening on medium-high speed until fluffy. Add the salt and coconut extract. Start the mixer on low, slowly increasing the speed to incorporate. Then mix on medium-high until light and fluffy. With the mixer on low speed, slowly add the powdered sugar and milk. Turn the mixer to medium-high and whip until fluffy.

7. Place 1 cake layer on a 10-inch cake round. Using a serrated knife, level off the top of the cake. Using an offset spatula, spread 1 cup of icing to the edges of the cake layer. Trim the second cake layer, set it on top of the icing, and repeat to ice that layer. Top with the remaining cake layer. Place a generous cup of icing on top of the cake and spread a very thin layer across the top, pushing as much of the icing as you can to the edges. Spread the icing at the edges of the top of the cake down and around the sides. Keep the icing layer very thin and always move the spatula through the icing, pushing it toward the unfrosted part. When the cake is completely iced, sprinkle the top with the toasted coconut.

8. Serve the cake at room temperature. Store, covered, in the refrigerator for up to 2 days.

Makes one 9-inch three-layer cake

Jo's Peanut Butter Balls

prep: *35 minutes, plus 10 minutes chilling*   **cook:** *10 minutes*   **cool:** *20 minutes*

It's a holiday tradition of our family's to spend a full day making candy that we package up to share with family and friends. I like to add sprinkles to the tops of these during the holidays. Every few years I'll switch up what we make, but I never can do without these Peanut Butter Balls. The kids love to help roll out each one, and I swear half don't even make it to the dipping bowl because the kids have already consumed the peanut butter filling.

7 tablespoons unsalted butter, at room temperature

2 cups peanut butter

2 cups powdered sugar

10 ounces marshmallows

1 teaspoon pure vanilla extract

6 cups Cocoa Krispies

24 ounces chocolate bark coating

1. Line a baking sheet with parchment paper.

2. In a stand mixer fitted with the paddle attachment on medium-high speed, cream 4 tablespoons of the butter, the peanut butter, and powdered sugar for 1 minute, until smooth.

3. In a 5-quart stock pot over medium heat, melt the remaining 3 tablespoons of butter. Add the marshmallows and vanilla and cook, stirring, until the marshmallows have melted. Add the peanut butter mixture and stir continually until the mixture is smooth. Add the cereal and stir until combined.

4. Form the mixture into 1½-inch balls and place them on the prepared baking sheet. Refrigerate them for about 10 minutes.

5. Meanwhile, follow the directions on the chocolate bark to melt it. Stir until smooth.

6. Using a fork, place a peanut butter ball in the melted chocolate and coat it fully, then set it back on the baking sheet. Repeat until all the balls have been dipped in chocolate coating.

7. Refrigerate again until the coating has hardened, about 20 minutes.

8. When cool, transfer the balls to an airtight container and refrigerate for up to 5 days.

Makes about 60 balls

Classic Cheesecake

prep: *20 minutes* **cook:** *1 hour 20 minutes* **cool:** *7 hours*

Graham Cracker Crust
(page 25)

Three 8-ounce blocks cream
cheese, at room temperature

½ cup sugar

¼ cup sour cream

2 tablespoons plus 1 teaspoon
cornstarch

3 large eggs

1 tablespoon fresh lemon juice

1 teaspoon pure vanilla extract

1¼ cups heavy cream

1. Preheat the oven to 350°F.

2. Double-wrap the bottom of a 9-inch springform pan with foil to keep water from seeping into the pan. Press the crust into the bottom of the pan and halfway up the sides.

3. Bake the crust until golden brown, 8 to 10 minutes. Remove from the oven but leave the oven on.

4. Meanwhile, in a stand mixer fitted with the paddle attachment, combine the cream cheese, sugar, sour cream, and cornstarch. Mix on medium-high speed until light and fluffy. Slowly beat in the eggs, lemon juice, and vanilla. Mix until thoroughly incorporated. Turn the mixer off and scrape down the sides of the bowl well. Pour in the cream and mix on low speed until the mixture is smooth.

5. Pour the filling into the baked crust.

6. Place the cheesecake in a baking pan that is larger than the springform pan and carefully fill the pan about three-quarters full with hot water.

7. Bake the cheesecake until the center only slightly jiggles, 1 hour to 1 hour 10 minutes.

8. When the cheesecake comes out of the oven, remove it from the water bath and place on a wire rack. Carefully run a thin knife around the edge of the cheesecake to release it from the sides of the pan. Let the cheesecake cool to room temperature for at least 1 hour, then remove the sides of the springform pan.

9. Refrigerate for at least 6 hours before serving. Cut into 8 to 10 slices.

10. Store loosely covered with plastic wrap in the refrigerator for up to 2 days.

Makes one 9-inch cheesecake

TIP: *If you like, garnish the cheesecake with strawberries.*

Aunt Mary's Cherry Mashers

prep: *45 minutes, plus under 2 hours chilling*   **cook:** *10 minutes*   **cool:** *20 minutes*

There is an unexpected delight that comes with the blend of cherry and chocolate. My dad's sister used to make these candies every year around the holidays, and his love for them became my own. I asked my aunt Mary if I could share her recipe in this book and she gladly obliged—and there's no doubt I'll be adding it to the lineup of treats I make every holiday season.

One 7.2-ounce package Betty Crocker Home Style Fluffy White Frosting Mix (see Note)

1 pound powdered sugar

6 tablespoons (¾ stick) margarine, at room temperature

One 10-ounce jar maraschino cherries, drained and chopped

½ teaspoon pure vanilla extract

¼ cup sweetened condensed milk

One 20-ounce package chocolate almond bark, broken into smaller pieces

One 11.5-ounce bag milk chocolate chips

2½ cups dry-roasted salted peanuts, finely chopped

1 tablespoon vegetable oil

1. Line a baking sheet with parchment paper.

2. In a stand mixer fitted with the paddle attachment, combine the frosting mix, powdered sugar, margarine, maraschino cherries, vanilla, and condensed milk. Starting on low speed, then gradually turning the speed to medium, beat until the mixture has a fluffy consistency, about 4 minutes.

3. Form the cherry mixture into 1-inch balls using a small (.75-ounce) cookie scoop. Place on the prepared baking sheet and freeze until firm, 1 to 2 hours.

4. To make the chocolate coating, in a medium saucepan, combine the chocolate bark, chocolate chips, peanuts, and vegetable oil and melt over medium heat, mixing to combine.

5. Working in batches, remove the cherry balls from the freezer and dunk them one at a time with a fork or spoon into the chocolate mixture. Allow any excess chocolate to drip off over the pan, then return the balls to the parchment paper.

6. Refrigerate until completely hardened, about 20 minutes.

7. Store in an airtight container in the refrigerator for up to 3 days.

NOTE: If you can't find or don't want to use the powdered frosting mix, omit the mix and decrease the amount of sweetened condensed milk to 3 tablespoons.

Makes about 4 dozen

Chocolate Soufflés

prep: *30 minutes*   **cook:** *under 15 minutes*   **cool:** *none*

2 tablespoons unsalted butter, melted

2 tablespoons granulated sugar

soufflés

2 ounces unsweetened chocolate, chopped

⅓ cup semisweet chocolate chips

3 tablespoons unsalted butter

⅓ cup plus 1 tablespoon bread flour or all-purpose flour

1 cup cold milk

6 large egg yolks

5 large egg whites

1 teaspoon pure vanilla extract

⅓ cup plus 1 tablespoon granulated sugar

¼ cup powdered sugar

1. Preheat the oven to 375°F. Line a baking sheet with parchment paper.

2. To prepare the ramekins: Brush the bottoms and sides of eight 5-ounce ramekins with the melted butter. Divide the granulated sugar among the ramekins and turn them to thoroughly coat the bottoms and sides. Discard any extra sugar.

3. To make the soufflés: In a small stainless steel bowl or the top of a double boiler, combine the chopped chocolate and chocolate chips. Nest the bowl over a pot of barely simmering water (the bowl should not touch the water) and stir the chocolate until melted (taking care not to get any water in the bowl). Set the bowl aside off the heat.

4. In a medium saucepan, melt the butter over medium heat. Sprinkle in the flour and whisk until the flour is incorporated and the mixture thickens, about 1 minute. Reduce the heat to low and whisk in the milk. Continue whisking until the mixture becomes smooth, 2 to 3 minutes. Remove the saucepan from the heat. Transfer the mixture to the bowl with the melted chocolate and stir to combine. Slowly stir the egg yolks into the chocolate mixture. Set aside.

5. In a bowl, with an electric mixer fitted with the whisk, whip the egg whites and vanilla until the whites start to get foamy, then sprinkle in the sugar. Continue whipping the egg whites on medium speed until they form soft peaks and the consistency resembles whipped cream, about 3 minutes.

6. Use a spatula to fold about one-third of the egg whites into the chocolate mixture, carefully lifting from the bottom and folding over. Fold in half the remaining egg whites, then the last of the egg whites, taking care not to deflate the mixture.

7. Divide the mixture among the prepared ramekins and place them on the prepared baking sheet.

8. Bake the soufflés undisturbed until they have risen over the top of the rims, 12 to 15 minutes.

9. Pour the powdered sugar into a sifter or fine-mesh sieve and gently tap over each soufflé immediately as it comes out of the oven.

10. Serve immediately.

Makes 8 servings

Tres Leches Cake

prep: *25 minutes, plus 1 hour chilling*   **cook:** *under 30 minutes*   **cool:** *2 hours*

Butter, for the pan

3 cups all-purpose flour

1 tablespoon baking powder

1 teaspoon kosher salt

6 large eggs, at room temperature

2 cups sugar

3 teaspoons pure vanilla extract

1 cup milk, at room temperature

2 cups heavy cream

One 12-ounce can evaporated milk

1 teaspoon ground cinnamon, plus more for sprinkling

One 14-ounce can sweetened condensed milk

Sliced fresh strawberries, whipped cream (see page 321), and mint leaves, for serving (optional)

1. Preheat the oven to 350°F. Lightly grease a 9 × 13-inch baking pan with butter.

2. In a medium bowl, mix together the flour, baking powder, and salt. Set aside.

3. In a stand mixer fitted with the paddle attachment, beat the eggs and sugar on medium-high speed until light and fluffy and the color is lightened, 6 to 7 minutes. Slowly add 2 teaspoons of the vanilla and mix until just combined.

4. With the mixer on low speed, add half of the flour mixture, then the milk, finishing with the remaining flour mixture, mixing well after each addition.

5. Pour the batter into the prepared pan and bake until a tester inserted into the center comes out clean, 23 to 28 minutes. Let the cake cool completely, approximately 1 hour.

6. Meanwhile, in a medium saucepan, whisk together the cream, evaporated milk, and cinnamon. Bring to a boil over medium heat, then reduce the heat and simmer for 2 minutes, stirring occasionally, until completely combined and smooth. Set aside for 5 to 8 minutes to let the flavors meld.

7. Whisk the sweetened condensed milk and the remaining 1 teaspoon vanilla into the cream mixture.

8. Using a fork, poke holes in the top of the cooled cake. Pour the cream mixture over the cake. Cover with plastic wrap and refrigerate for at least 2 hours or overnight.

9. Slice and sprinkle each serving with cinnamon. Serve with sliced strawberries, whipped cream, and fresh mint leaves, if desired.

10. Store covered in the refrigerator for up to 3 days.

Makes one 9 × 13-inch cake

Crème Brûlée

WITH FRESH BERRIES

prep: *35 minutes, plus 2 hours 20 minutes chilling*   **cook:** *40 minutes*   **cool:** *5 minutes*

1 quart heavy cream

2 vanilla beans, split lengthwise

1 cup sugar

6 large egg yolks

8 cups hot water

Fresh berries, for serving

1. Preheat the oven 325°F.

2. Place the cream in a medium saucepan, scrape the vanilla seeds into the cream and throw in the vanilla pods, too. Bring to a light boil over medium heat, remove from the heat, and let cool slightly, 15 to 20 minutes. Remove the vanilla pods and set the cream aside to cool.

3. In a large bowl, whisk together ¾ cup of the sugar and the egg yolks until light and fluffy, 2 to 3 minutes. Slowly add the cooled cream mixture, whisking constantly until smooth.

4. Divide the mixture among six 6- to 8-ounce ramekins. Place them in a roasting pan that is 3 to 4 inches deep and large enough to allow 1 to 2 inches between the ramekins.

5. Carefully (so as not to splash into the ramekins) pour the hot water into the pan to come halfway up the sides of the ramekins.

6. Bake until the custard is set but still slightly jiggles when touched, about 40 minutes.

7. Remove the ramekins from the water bath and let them cool to room temperature. Chill in the fridge for at least 2 hours.

8. Using the remaining ¼ cup sugar, sprinkle an even layer over the crème brûlées (about ½ tablespoon per ramekin). Use a kitchen torch to heat the sugar until melted and browned. Let cool for 5 minutes before serving.

9. Top with fresh berries and serve at room temperature.

Makes 6 servings

Strawberry Pie

prep: *20 minutes*   **cook:** *none*   **cool:** *6 hours*

¾ cup plus 2 tablespoons (7 ounces) sweetened condensed milk

2 tablespoons fresh lemon juice

2 cups (about 9 ounces) strawberries, hulled and cut into ¼-inch dice (about 1½ cups), plus whole strawberries, for garnish (optional)

1 cup heavy cream

1 teaspoon pure vanilla extract

¼ cup powdered sugar

Graham Cracker Crust (page 25)

1. In a large bowl, whisk together the condensed milk and lemon juice, then stir in the diced strawberries.

2. In a stand mixer fitted with the whisk attachment, mix the heavy cream, vanilla extract, and powdered sugar on a low speed for 30 seconds. Increase the speed to medium-high and beat until stiff peaks form, about 2 minutes.

3. Add the whipped cream to the bowl with the condensed milk mixture, and gently fold it in. The consistency will resemble a thick pudding. Pour the pie filling into the crust.

4. Freeze for at least 6 hours or up to overnight. Garnish with strawberries, if desired.

5. Remove from the freezer and serve immediately.

6. Store, covered, in the freezer for up to 5 days.

Makes one 9-inch pie

Magnolia Press Chocolate Cake

prep: *45 minutes, plus 1 hour 15 minutes chilling*   **cook:** *35 minutes*   **cool:** *30 minutes*

continued . . .

cake

Nonstick baking spray

1¼ cups (2½ sticks) unsalted butter, at room temperature

1½ cups granulated sugar

2 large eggs

2 teaspoons pure vanilla extract

2 cups all-purpose flour

⅔ cup unsweetened cocoa powder

2 teaspoons baking soda

½ teaspoon kosher salt

1½ cups hot strong-brewed coffee

2 teaspoons distilled white vinegar

filling

4 tablespoons (½ stick) unsalted butter, at room temperature

¼ cup vegetable shortening

½ teaspoon pure vanilla extract

½ cup powdered sugar, sifted

2 tablespoons whole milk

1. To make the cake: Preheat the oven to 350°F. Heavily spray a 9 × 13-inch baking pan with nonstick baking spray. Line the bottom of the pan with a rectangle of parchment paper and lightly spray the paper.

2. In a stand mixer fitted with the paddle attachment, beat the butter and granulated sugar on medium speed until creamy, about 1 minute. Add the eggs one at a time, beating just until mixed in after each addition. Beat in the vanilla.

3. In a medium bowl, combine the flour, cocoa, baking soda, and salt. Add to the butter mixture, alternating and ending with the coffee, and beat until blended. Stir in the vinegar.

4. Pour the batter into the prepared pan. Bake until a tester inserted in the center comes out clean, 23 to 28 minutes. Cool in the pan on a wire rack for 15 minutes, then place the rack on top of the cake and invert the cake onto the rack to cool completely, about 1 hour.

5. To make the filling: In a stand mixer fitted with the paddle attachment, beat the butter and shortening on medium-high speed until light and fluffy, about 2 minutes. Reduce the speed to low and beat in the vanilla until combined. Gradually add the powdered sugar and milk until thoroughly combined. Increase the speed to medium and beat until fluffy, 2 to 3 minutes.

6. Transfer the filling to a piping bag or a heavy-duty zip-top plastic bag and snip a ½-inch hole in the tip. Set aside.

7. Use a 2½-inch round cutter to cut 12 rounds from the cake. Use a 1-inch round cutter to cut about 1 inch deep into the center of each of the little cakes, taking care not to go all the way through. Carefully remove the centers to leave a 1-inch-deep hole in the center of each cake. Slice off the top ¼ inch of the 1-inch center pieces and set aside to use as lids.

continued from page 299

chocolate glaze

8 ounces bittersweet
  chocolate baking bars,
  chopped

8 tablespoons (1 stick)
  unsalted butter, cut into
  8 pieces

1 tablespoon light corn syrup

8. Use the piping bag to fill the center of each cake with about 2 teaspoons of filling per cake, leaving a very small space at the top of each one. Place a reserved ¼-inch round cutout on top of the filling of each cake, pressing down lightly to secure. Put the cakes on a wire rack set over a large sheet pan.

9. To make the chocolate glaze: In a 1-quart microwave-safe glass measuring cup (this will make it easy to pour the glaze over the cakes), combine the bittersweet chocolate and butter. Microwave on medium (50%) power in 30-second increments, stirring after each, until melted, 2 to 3 minutes. Stir in the corn syrup and microwave for about 1 minute, stirring every 30 seconds, until the mixture is smooth and glossy.

10. Working quickly, carefully pour the glaze over each cake, smoothing the glaze toward the edges and around the sides using a small offset spatula. Chill the glazed cakes for at least 30 minutes to set.

11. Store in an airtight container in the refrigerator for up to 3 days.

Makes 12 cakes

Linnie Mae's Pound Cake

prep: *15 minutes*   **cook:** *1 hour 5 minutes*   **cool:** *20 minutes*

Linnie Mae is a longtime friend of Chip's parents, and her lemon vanilla pound cake is something of a legend in Archer City, Texas, the small town she calls home. The first time she made it was to help ease her grief as she mourned the loss of her daughter. The comfort she found in baking began a tradition that Linnie Mae continues today: baking cakes as a simple act of hospitality for a family in need or to lift a neighbor's spirits. The people of her town seem to know its value—in fact, one year Linnie Mae made two pound cakes for a local charity auction, and they sold for $6,000! The cake itself lives up to the hype—always moist and never too sweet. The most important ingredient, according to Linnie Mae, is the amount of love you bake right in.

Nonstick baking spray

1 cup (2 sticks) unsalted butter, at room temperature

3 cups sugar

6 large eggs

2 teaspoons pure vanilla extract

1 teaspoon almond extract

2 teaspoons lemon extract

2 teaspoons butter extract

3 cups all-purpose flour

½ teaspoon kosher salt

¼ teaspoon baking soda

1 cup buttermilk

1. Preheat the oven to 325°F. Spray a standard Bundt pan with nonstick baking spray.

2. In a stand mixer fitted with the paddle attachment, cream the butter and sugar on medium-high speed until light and fluffy, about 2 minutes. Add the eggs one at a time, beating well after each addition. Add the extracts and mix until smooth.

3. In a medium bowl, whisk together the flour, salt, and baking soda. On low speed, add the flour in three additions, alternating with the buttermilk, beginning and ending with the flour. Mix until fully incorporated.

4. Pour the batter into the prepared pan and spread it out evenly. Bake until golden brown and a tester inserted into the center comes out clean, 1 hour to 1 hour 5 minutes. Cool for 20 minutes on a wire rack, then unmold the cake onto the rack.

5. Store in an airtight container at room temperature for up to 3 days.

Makes one 10-cup Bundt cake

TIP: *Serve with strawberries and whipped cream, or warm with jelly in the morning.*

Double-Crusted Key Lime Pie

prep: *15 minutes*   **cook:** *25 minutes*   **cool:** *3 hours*

2 cups cinnamon-flavored graham cracker crumbs

6 tablespoons (¾ stick) unsalted butter, melted

4 large egg yolks

1 large egg

One 14-ounce can sweetened condensed milk

½ cup fresh lime juice, preferably from Key limes

1 teaspoon grated lime zest, plus more for garnish

Whipped cream (see page 321), for serving

1. Preheat the oven to 350°F.

2. In a medium bowl, combine the graham cracker crumbs and melted butter. Mix until the crumbs are well coated.

3. Press into a 9-inch glass pie plate and bake until the crust is set, about 10 minutes. Set aside to cool slightly for 10 minutes. Leave the oven on.

4. Meanwhile, in a large bowl, whisk together the egg yolks, whole egg, condensed milk, lime juice, and lime zest until well incorporated.

5. Pour the filling into the slightly cooled pie crust. Return to the oven and bake until just set, about 14 minutes. Remove from the oven and let cool completely on a wire rack, about 1 hour.

6. Refrigerate until chilled, about 2 hours.

7. Top with lime zest and whipped cream to serve.

Makes one 9-inch pie

Oatmeal Cream Pies

prep: *35 minutes, plus 20 minutes chilling*   **cook:** *30 minutes*   **cool:** *30 minutes*

The last day of the school year for my kids is always a celebrated transition in our house. As a way to both honor the kids' school year and officially declare the start of summer, I'll throw together pretty much every kind of food that embodies summer to my kids: watermelon, corn on the cob, barbecue, potato salad, and of course, these sweet little oatmeal cream pies. Every year when I make them, they remind me of my own childhood, and it's safe to say that my kids love them just as much as I did.

cookies

1¼ cups (2½ sticks) unsalted butter, at room temperature

1 cup packed dark brown sugar

½ cup granulated sugar

1 large egg, at room temperature

2 teaspoons pure vanilla extract

1 teaspoon dark molasses

1½ cups all-purpose flour

1 teaspoon baking soda

½ teaspoon kosher salt

¼ teaspoon ground cinnamon

3 cups quick-cooking oats

filling

¾ cup (1½ sticks) unsalted butter, at room temperature

1 teaspoon pure vanilla extract

2½ cups powdered sugar

1 tablespoon milk

1. Preheat the oven to 375°F. Line three large baking sheets with parchment paper.

2. In a stand mixer fitted with the paddle attachment, cream the butter, brown sugar, and granulated sugar on medium speed until light and fluffy, about 2 minutes. Slowly beat in the egg, vanilla, and molasses and mix until smooth, scraping down the sides as needed.

3. In a medium bowl, whisk together the flour, baking soda, salt, cinnamon, and oats until combined. On low speed, add the oat mixture to the creamed butter mixture about ⅓ cup at a time, beating until combined.

4. Using a 1½-tablespoon scoop to portion the dough, place the dough balls about 2 inches apart on the baking sheets (10 cookies per sheet).

5. Refrigerate the baking sheets for at least 20 minutes.

6. One sheet at a time, bake the cookies until lightly golden, 10 to 12 minutes. Let the cookies cool on the baking sheet on a wire rack for 30 minutes.

7. In a stand mixer fitted with the paddle attachment, cream the butter on high speed until light and fluffy, 3 to 4 minutes. Beat in the vanilla.

8. On low speed, slowly beat in the powdered sugar, about ¼ cup at a time. Then beat in the milk. When the mixture is smooth, increase the speed to medium, mixing until thoroughly combined and fluffy, about 2 minutes.

9. Set the cookies up in pairs, with the bottom of one of them facing up. Using a small (1-tablespoon) scoop, place filling on the bottom of the upside-down cookie. Place the second cookie on top, right side up, and sandwich them together, pressing just enough to spread the filling to the edges. Repeat to make the rest of the sandwiches.

Makes 15 sandwich cookies

Flourless Chocolate Cake

prep: *20 minutes, plus 10 minutes cooling*   **cook:** *under 30 minutes*   **cool:** *1 hour*

cake

Nonstick baking spray

8 tablespoons (1 stick) unsalted butter

1 cup semisweet chocolate chips

¾ cup sugar

½ teaspoon kosher salt

1 tablespoon espresso powder

1 teaspoon pure vanilla extract

3 large eggs

½ cup unsweetened cocoa powder

ganache

1 cup semisweet chocolate chips

½ teaspoon pure vanilla extract

½ cup heavy cream

1. To make the cake: Preheat the oven to 375°F. Spray a 9-inch cake pan with nonstick baking spray. Line the bottom of the pan with a round of parchment paper and spray the paper with nonstick baking spray.

2. In a small saucepan, combine the butter and chocolate chips and melt over low heat.

3. Pour the chocolate mixture into a medium bowl, then add the sugar, salt, espresso powder, vanilla, and eggs. Whisk until the batter is smooth. Add the cocoa and whisk until just incorporated.

4. Pour the batter into the prepared cake pan and spread it out evenly. Bake until a tester inserted in the center comes out clean, 24 to 26 minutes.

5. Cool in the pan for 10 minutes, then unmold onto a wire rack to cool completely.

6. To make the ganache: In a medium bowl, combine the chocolate chips and vanilla. In a small microwave-safe bowl, warm the cream for about 45 seconds to 1 minute. The cream should be hot but not bubbling. Pour the hot cream over the chocolate chip mixture and let sit for about 3 minutes, until the chips are mostly melted. Whisk until the mixture is completely smooth.

7. Spoon the ganache over the completely cooled cake, spreading it out to cover the cake and drip over the edges. Let stand for at least 1 hour to allow the ganache to set. (If you can't wait an hour, refrigerate for 30 minutes to set.)

8. Store in an airtight container at room temperature for up to 2 days.

Makes one 9-inch cake

Lemon Lavender Tart

prep: *20 minutes, plus 30 minutes cooling*   **cook:** *40 minutes*   **cool:** *2 hours*

Homemade Pie Crust (page 23) or Tart Shell (page 27), or 1 store-bought refrigerated pie crust

lemon curd

2 large eggs

2 large egg yolks

¾ cup sugar

2 teaspoons grated lemon zest

⅓ cup fresh lemon juice

½ teaspoon ground lavender

2 tablespoons heavy cream

8 tablespoons (1 stick) unsalted butter, cut into pieces

Whipped cream (see page 321) for serving (optional)

1. Fit the dough into an 8-inch tart pan, preferably with a removable bottom, and blind bake according to the recipe (for the homemade doughs) or the package directions for the store-bought. Set aside to cool until ready to fill.

2. In a medium stainless steel bowl or the top of a double boiler, whisk together the whole eggs, egg yolks, sugar, lemon zest, lemon juice, lavender, and cream until well combined, about 1 minute.

3. Nest the bowl over a pot of simmering water (the bowl should not touch the water) and whisk constantly while cooking until the mixture becomes thick, 15 to 20 minutes. It should coat the back of a spoon.

4. Remove the bowl from the heat and whisk vigorously for 30 seconds to release some heat. Set a fine-mesh sieve over another bowl and strain the lemon mixture immediately through the sieve into the second bowl. Add the butter and whisk until smooth and shiny, 2 to 3 minutes. Let the mixture cool completely. (This lemon curd filling may be made ahead and stored covered in the refrigerator for up to 5 days.)

5. Pour the filling into the tart shell and spread it out evenly. Refrigerate for at least 2 hours to set before serving.

6. Slice and serve with whipped cream, if desired.

7. Store covered in the refrigerator for up to 3 days.

Makes 6 to 8 servings

TIP: *Garnish with lavender flowers, if desired.*

Aunt Opal's Coconut Cream Pie

prep: *30 minutes, plus 2 hours chilling*   **cook:** *35 minutes*   **cool:** *45 minutes*

Chip's aunt Opal and her husband, Curly, owned a small restaurant in Archer City, Texas, known for its homemade desserts. You may be familiar with Aunt Opal's Banana Pudding, which I had in my first cookbook. Every dessert I've ever tasted from her collection of recipes has been so delicious, I knew I had to share another here.

filling

⅔ cup sugar

¼ cup cornstarch

½ teaspoon kosher salt

3 cups whole milk

4 large egg yolks

1 tablespoon unsalted butter

1½ teaspoons pure vanilla extract

½ teaspoon coconut extract

½ cup sweetened shredded coconut

1 prebaked 9-inch pie crust, homemade (page 23) or store-bought

meringue

3 large egg whites, at room temperature

¼ teaspoon cream of tartar

6 tablespoons sugar

½ teaspoon pure vanilla extract

1. To make the filling: In a medium saucepan, combine the sugar, cornstarch, and salt. Gradually whisk in the milk and bring to a simmer over medium heat, whisking occasionally. Remove from the heat.

2. In a medium bowl, lightly whisk the egg yolks. Slowly add half of the hot milk mixture, whisking constantly, then whisk in the rest. Return the mixture to the saucepan and bring it to a boil over medium heat. Cook, whisking constantly, until the mixture thickens, about 1 minute. It should have the consistency of pudding.

3. Remove from the heat and stir in the butter, vanilla, coconut extract, and shredded coconut.

4. Pour the filling into the prepared pie crust. Place plastic wrap directly over the filling to keep it from forming a "skin." Refrigerate until well chilled, about 2 hours.

5. When the pie is fully chilled, preheat the oven to 350°F.

6. Meanwhile, to make the meringue: In a medium bowl, with an electric mixer fitted with the whisk, whip the egg whites on medium-low speed until frothy, then add the cream of tartar. Increase the speed to medium-high and whip until fluffy, about 1 minute. With the mixer running, slowly add the sugar. Continue whipping until the mixture becomes glossy and holds stiff peaks, about 4 minutes. Add the vanilla and mix gently and thoroughly.

7. Top the entire pie filling with the meringue.

8. Bake until the meringue begins to brown, about 15 minutes.

9. Let cool, then refrigerate until chilled, about 45 minutes. Store in the refrigerator for up to 2 days.

Makes one 9-inch pie

Chewy Granola Bars

prep: *20 minutes, plus 10 minutes cooling*   **cook:** *20 minutes*   **cool:** *2 hours*

2 cups rolled oats

1 cup sliced almonds

1 cup loosely packed unsweetened shredded coconut

1½ cups dried cherries

½ cup honey

¼ cup lightly packed light brown sugar

3 tablespoons unsalted butter

¼ teaspoon kosher salt

½ vanilla bean, split lengthwise

⅓ cup mini semisweet chocolate chips

1. Preheat the oven to 325°F. Line a sheet pan with parchment paper.

2. Spread the oats and almonds on the pan and bake until the almonds are fragrant, about 10 minutes. Add the coconut and bake until the coconut and oats are lightly toasted and the almonds are golden, about 5 minutes longer. Pour the mixture into a large heatproof bowl and add the cherries.

3. In a small saucepan, combine the honey, brown sugar, butter, and salt. Scrape the vanilla seeds into the pan and add the vanilla pod. Cook over medium heat, stirring occasionally, until the butter is melted and the sugar is dissolved, about 5 minutes. Set aside to cool for 10 to 15 minutes. Carefully remove the vanilla pod, using a small knife to scrape any remaining seeds into the pan.

4. Pour the honey mixture over the oat mixture and stir to combine. Add half the chocolate chips and stir to combine.

5. Line a 9 × 13-inch baking dish with parchment paper, allowing the paper to extend past the sides to use as a lift later. Spread the mixture into the dish and press down with the back of a silicone spatula. Sprinkle the remaining chocolate chips over the mixture and press firmly to set.

6. Refrigerate for at least 2 hours.

7. Lift the block from the pan using the parchment and place it on a cutting board. Cut the block into squares or other desired shapes or crumble and use to top vanilla ice cream.

Makes 10 to 12 servings

Silo Cookies

prep: *25 minutes, plus 30 minutes chilling*   **cook:** *under 45 minutes*   **cool:** *10 minutes*

The credit for this recipe really belongs to Chip and the kids. They each have a different favorite cookie, so one day, I dumped in everyone's must-have ingredient: nuts for Chip, peanut butter for the girls, and chocolate for the boys. It was a complete win across the board. So it became our family's signature cookie, and the first item on the menu when we opened Silos Baking Co.

1 cup (2 sticks) unsalted butter, at room temperature

1 cup packed light brown sugar

¾ cup granulated sugar

2 large eggs

2 teaspoons pure vanilla extract

2 cups all-purpose flour

1 teaspoon kosher salt

1 teaspoon baking soda

1½ cups rolled oats

1½ cups semisweet chocolate chips

1½ cups peanut butter chips

½ cup chopped walnuts

1. Preheat the oven to 350°F. Line two baking sheets with parchment paper.

2. In a stand mixer fitted with the paddle attachment, cream the butter, brown sugar, and granulated sugar on medium speed until light and fluffy, about 4 minutes. Reduce the speed to medium-low and add the eggs one at a time, beating until blended after each addition. Add the vanilla and beat until well incorporated.

3. In a medium bowl, whisk together the flour, salt, and baking soda. Slowly add the flour mixture to the mixer and beat until incorporated. Reduce the speed to low, add the oats, chocolate chips, peanut butter chips, and walnuts and beat until incorporated, 15 to 20 seconds.

4. Using a 2-ounce cookie scoop, scoop the dough onto one of the prepared baking sheets, placing the scoops side by side. Refrigerate for at least 30 minutes.

5. Baking in batches, and leaving the dough balls in the refrigerator until needed, set the dough balls 3 inches apart on the second prepared baking sheet and bake until browned, 13 to 15 minutes. Let cool on the baking sheet for about 10 minutes. Repeat with the remaining cookies.

6. Store in an airtight container at room temperature for up to 5 days.

Makes 18 cookies

Dessert Crêpes

prep: *15 minutes, plus 20 minutes chilling*   **cook:** *15 minutes*   **cool:** *none*

When I make dessert crêpes, I like to set them up self-serve style with a variety of fillings, including strawberries, Nutella, banana, and whipped cream so everyone can tailor their own. The crêpe itself is so light and thin that you won't feel guilty about having more than one . . . or three (there's no judgment here!).

crêpes

1 cup all-purpose flour

2 large eggs

¾ cup whole milk

½ cup water

2 tablespoons granulated sugar

1 teaspoon pure vanilla extract

½ teaspoon kosher salt

3 tablespoons unsalted butter, melted

filling suggestions

Macerated strawberries

Lemon curd (see page 309)

Sliced bananas and ground cinnamon

Whipped cream (see page 321) with fresh berries

Nutella

garnish

¼ cup powdered sugar, sifted, for dusting

1. To make the crêpes: In a blender, combine the flour, eggs, milk, water, sugar, vanilla, salt, and butter and pulse to combine for about 1 minute. Let the batter sit in the fridge to rest for at least 20 minutes or overnight.

2. Heat a dry nonstick medium skillet over medium heat for about 3 minutes. Pour about ¼ cup of the batter into the center of the pan and tilt in a circle to thin it out. Cook for 20 to 30 seconds, carefully flip the crêpe using a spatula, and cook for another 10 seconds. Remove the crêpe and lay it on a plate. Repeat to make more crêpes, working quickly but gently, to avoid tearing. Stack the crêpes on the plate to keep them warm.

3. Fill the crêpes with your filling of choice and roll up carefully. Dust with powdered sugar and serve.

Makes 10 to 12 servings

Crew's Cookies

prep: *1 hour, plus 1 hour chilling*   **cook:** *under 40 minutes*   **cool:** *1 hour*

Crew tagged along for the final recipe tasting for this book—and when these cookies hit the table, he had more than his fair share. This cookie has such a classic flavor that it makes for a really versatile treat—one that can be served as a simple dessert or an afternoon snack for the kids.

cookies

¾ cup (1½ sticks) unsalted butter, at room temperature

¾ cup granulated sugar

1 large egg

2 teaspoons pure vanilla extract

2¼ cups all-purpose flour

1 teaspoon ground cinnamon

½ teaspoon baking powder

½ teaspoon kosher salt

glaze

2 cups powdered sugar

½ to ¾ cup heavy cream

½ teaspoon pure vanilla extract

1. To make the cookies: In a stand mixer fitted with the paddle attachment, cream the butter and granulated sugar on medium-high speed until light and fluffy, 3 to 4 minutes. Add the egg and vanilla and beat on medium-high until well incorporated, about 30 seconds.

2. In a large bowl, whisk together the flour, cinnamon, baking powder, and salt.

3. On low speed, slowly add the flour mixture to the butter mixture. Mix until all the ingredients come together; a dough should be forming on the paddle and not sticking to the sides of your bowl.

4. Place the dough between 2 sheets of parchment paper and roll to about a ¼-inch thickness. Remove the top parchment sheet and use a 2-inch fluted round cookie cutter to cut out as many cookies as possible, leaving them in place. Gently peel off as much of the excess dough from between the cutout cookies as you can.

5. Carefully transfer the cut dough on the parchment from the work table to a baking sheet by gently sliding the parchment onto the baking sheet. Refrigerate for at least 30 minutes. This will firm up the dough and help you remove any remaining excess dough. Reroll the dough scraps and cut out more cookies.

6. Meanwhile, preheat the oven to 350°F.

7. Bake one baking sheet at a time until the edges of the cookies are slightly golden, 10 to 12 minutes, rotating the baking sheet front to back halfway through the baking time. Transfer the cookies to a wire rack to cool completely before glazing, about 30 minutes.

8. To make the glaze: In a medium bowl, whisk together the powdered sugar, ½ cup of the cream, and the vanilla. Mix in the remaining cream 1 tablespoon at a time until the glaze is the consistency of glue. (Drizzle a

continued . . .

continued from page 319

spoonful of the glaze back into the bowl and it should hold a ribbon for about 10 seconds before melting into itself.)

9. Transfer the glaze to a piping bag fitted with a small round tip or a heavy-duty zip-top bag with the corner snipped off. Pipe the glaze in a spiral on each cookie, starting in the middle and leaving a ¼-inch border around the edges. Use a toothpick to smooth the glaze, if needed. Let stand until the glaze hardens, about 1 hour.

10. Store in an airtight container at room temperature for up to 5 days.

Makes about 3 dozen cookies

TIP: *Baking chilled cookies helps maintain the perfect shape of Crew's Cookies.*

Black Forest Cake

prep: *1 hour 40 minutes*   **cook:** *under 30 minutes*   **cool:** *1 hour*

This is my dad's favorite cake, and it's the only thing he asks for on his birthday, year after year. For those of you who share a love for chocolate and cherry, you know it's a winning combination.

cake

Nonstick baking spray

2 cups granulated sugar

2¼ cups all-purpose flour

¾ cup unsweetened cocoa
  powder

1½ teaspoons baking powder

1½ teaspoons baking soda

1 teaspoon kosher salt

2 large eggs

1 cup whole milk

½ cup vegetable oil

2 teaspoons pure vanilla
  extract

2 teaspoons instant coffee
  crystals

1 cup hot water

filling

One 14.5-ounce can cherries

⅔ cup granulated sugar

3 tablespoons cornstarch

1 tablespoon unsalted butter

¼ teaspoon almond extract

whipped cream

1 pint heavy cream

¼ cup powdered sugar

1 teaspoon pure vanilla extract

1. To make the cake: Preheat the oven to 350°F. Spray three 8-inch round pans with nonstick baking spray.

2. In a large bowl, whisk together the granulated sugar, flour, cocoa, baking powder, baking soda, and salt.

3. In a stand mixer fitted with the whisk attachment, combine the eggs, milk, oil, and vanilla and whisk on medium speed until well combined, 1 to 2 minutes. On low speed, slowly add the flour mixture and mix until combined.

4. In a small bowl, stir the coffee crystals into the hot water. With the machine on low, slowly pour the coffee mixture into the mixer. Turn the mixer to medium speed and whisk until the batter is smooth, 1 to 2 minutes.

5. Divide the batter evenly among the three pans. Bake until a tester inserted in the center comes out clean, about 22 minutes. Let the cake layers cool in the pans on wire racks for 10 minutes, then unmold them onto the racks to cool completely. The cake layers must be completely cooled before you assemble the cake.

6. To make the filling: Drain the cherries, reserving ¼ cup of juice. In a large saucepan, combine the cherries and reserved juice, granulated sugar, and cornstarch. Bring the mixture to a boil over medium heat, stirring constantly. Reduce the heat and simmer until the juices begin to thicken, about 7 minutes. Stir in the butter and almond extract and set aside to cool to lukewarm.

7. To make the whipped cream: In a stand mixer fitted with the whisk attachment, combine the cream, powdered sugar, and vanilla. Start on low speed, then slowly turn the mixer up to high speed and continue mixing on high for 2 to 3 minutes until fluffy and the cream holds a soft peak when you pull the whisk out of the bowl.

8. Set one cake layer on an 8-inch cake round. Using a serrated knife, cut off the uneven top of the cake so that it's level, reserving the scraps. Using a

continued . . .

continued from page 321

piping bag fitted with a star tip, pipe the whipped cream to make a 2-inch-thick border around the top of the cake, starting at the outside edge and moving in. Spoon ⅓ cup cherry filling onto the center of the cake and gently spread it out to meet the whipped cream.

9. Add a second cake layer and level the top, again reserving the scraps. Repeat to make a whipped cream border with ⅓ cup cherry filling in the middle.

10. Lay the third layer on the cake. Add a generous cup of whipped cream to the top of the cake and spread to cover the top and sides. Keep the whipped cream layer thick enough to cover the cake, and always move the spatula through the whipped cream, pushing it toward the unfrosted part.

11. Turn the cake scraps into crumbs. Gently press cake crumbs into the whipped cream on the side of the cake. Spoon the remaining cherry filling onto the center of the top of the cake and pipe a border of whipped cream around the edge of the cake to keep the filling from leaking.

12. Refrigerate for 1 hour before serving. Serve cold.

13. Store in the refrigerator for up to 2 days.

Makes one 8-inch three-layer cake

acknowledgments

I can definitely say my family was not disappointed when they heard that a second cookbook was in the works. To them, it meant more food on the table, and even better, more dessert. So, first and foremost, thank you to Chip and the kids for being my biggest cheerleaders and most honest taste testers.

When it came time to build out a second book of recipes, the phrase "it takes a village" never felt more true, and I'm so grateful to everyone who helped bring this book to life.

Thank you to my home team at Magnolia.
To our team of recipe developers and all-around food experts: Becki Shepherd, Jamie Flanagan, Nicole McDuffie, and Holly Robb.
To the editorial team: Alissa Neely, Kelsie Monsen, Billy Jack Brawner, and Whitney Kaufhold. And to Kaila Luna, thank you for helping me articulate my thoughts and share my heart on these pages.
To those who kept us on track and pitched in for everything in between: Heidi Spring, Danielle Jackson, Becca Flannery, and Allison McGrane.

Thank you to the talented people who brought so much beauty to each page, through photography, styling, illustrations, and content: Amy Neunsinger, Frances Boswell, Kate Martindale, Andre Junget, and Shelli McConnell.

Thank you to Allison Lowery, Katie Barreira, and the amazing team at Meredith Publishing for helping us get all the recipes across the finish line.

Thank you to Cassie Jones and the team at William Morrow/ HarperCollins for your dedication and willingness to go above and beyond each step of the way.

And to all of you who have made my family's favorite meals a part of the fabric of your own families. Thank you for showing me what a gift it is to share and exchange stories and traditions around the table.

universal conversion chart

oven temperature equivalents

250°F = 120°C

275°F = 135°C

300°F = 150°C

325°F = 160°C

350°F = 180°C

375°F = 190°C

400°F = 200°C

425°F = 220°C

450°F = 230°C

475°F = 240°C

500°F = 260°C

measurement equivalents

*Measurements should always be level
unless directed otherwise.*

⅛ teaspoon = 0.5 mL

¼ teaspoon = 1 mL

½ teaspoon = 2 mL

1 teaspoon = 5 mL

1 tablespoon = 3 teaspoons = ½ fluid ounce = 15 mL

2 tablespoons = ⅛ cup = 1 fluid ounce = 30 mL

4 tablespoons = ¼ cup = 2 fluid ounces = 60 mL

5⅓ tablespoons = ⅓ cup = 3 fluid ounces = 80 mL

8 tablespoons = ½ cup = 4 fluid ounces = 120 mL

10⅔ tablespoons = ⅔ cup = 5 fluid ounces = 160 mL

12 tablespoons = ¾ cup = 6 fluid ounces = 180 mL

16 tablespoons = 1 cup = 8 fluid ounces = 240 mL

index

Note: Page references in *italics* indicate photographs.

Recipe Notes

Recipe Notes

Recipe Notes

Recipe Notes